Participants and Participation

PRAEGER SPECIAL STUDIES IN
U.S. ECONOMIC AND SOCIAL DEVELOPMENT

Participants and Participation

A STUDY OF SCHOOL POLICY IN NEW YORK CITY

Marilyn Gittell

Published in cooperation with
the Center for Urban Education

FREDERICK A. PRAEGER, Publishers
New York · Washington · London

To IRWIN, AMY, and ROSS

Foreword

Once upon a time, the people created public schools, and the schools belonged to them.

The people still pay for public education, and it is from them that the schools draw continuing sanction. But it is a myth that sanction and support add up to control. The reality is that control of public education in our large cities has passed over almost exclusively to management. Large-city school systems have taken on the shape of massive corporate enterprises, increasingly distant from the public.

Myth and reality are now beginning to clash. The shareholders and customers of American public education are restive. From determined, increasingly sophisticated parent groups in middle-class suburbs to angry rump boards of education in New York City's ghettos, the public is seeking to repossess its schools, or at least to establish a beachhead from which it can call the schools to account for their performance.

The first step in this developing revolt is an understanding of the dynamics of power in public-school systems, and in *Participants and Participation,* Marilyn Gittell has given us a lucid travel guide to the colossus of them all, the New York City public schools. The essential point of Dr. Gittell's careful tour through a labyrinth of decision making and authority is that the City's $1 billion-a-year, one-million pupil, 50,000-teacher school enterprise is a closed system. Not only has the public been shut out, but so have the agents closest to the child — the parent and the teacher. "Any effort to change the school system and expand civic participation," Dr. Gittell writes, "must face the concentration of power in the professional bureaucracy and the resistance by the bureaucracy to any plan that would erode its power."

Many educators will be surprised, as I was, to discover that the author is not an educator who has acquired some of the tools of political science but, rather, a political scientist who has mastered the anatomy of a school system. And simmering just below the surface of her clinical analysis is a sensitivity to the human forces — drives for power, on the one hand, and apathy and frustration bred by a closed system, on the other.

Unfortunately, some educators will read this study defensively, for it deals with some painful truths. But the truth of the matter is that educators dedicated to their profession and craft should welcome such scholarly invasions of their turf because many teachers and school administrators are themselves thwarted by the polarization of power in the public schools. As the school system has drifted away from the public, inbreeding has increased. Personnel and policy decisions have become unduly influenced by the sway of one or another ethnic or vested interest group. A mood of indecision as well as of isolation is increasingly prevalent. Some critics have plainly declared the system bankrupt, and the most aggrieved creditors are the children.

If this is the way it is, what is the way out? "Any plan for change must have as its first objective the diminution of bureaucratic power," says Dr. Gittell. "Meaningful plans for the reorganization of large city school systems must embody a formula for bureaucratic authority and the expansion of outside nonprofessional influences....Greater reliance on more local involvement through decentralization is the most natural approach to such...reorganization."

Her plea is not a cry in the wilderness. In New York City, a drive is under way for greater community participation in public education. The Board of Education itself adopted a decentralization plan of sorts in the spring of 1967, and a 1967 act of the state legislature called for school reorganization, declaring: "Increased community awareness and participation in the educational process is essential to the furtherance of educational innovation and excellence in the public school system within the city of New York."

For a long time, a few thoughtful educators have argued that education can be strengthened by linking the schools intimately to a system of political accountability, not by a pristine detachment from political processes. Thus, in 1928, in a pioneering study of the Chicago public schools, George S. Counts recommended:

> *Rather than seek refuge in the cautious counsel of removing the school from politics, we should move forward under the assumption that the real business of politics is to provide the channels through which the living energies of society may flow into new forms and patterns. The great desideratum...is to devise some means of making the school responsive to the more fundamental social realities and of enabling it at the same time to maintain an even keel amid the clash and roar of the contending elements.*

Four decades later, we may finally be drawing the schools closer to the community they are supposed to serve.

Dr. Gittell is a scholar engaged. Her venture into the corridors of power in the New York City school system began with her staff work for New York's Temporary Commission on City Finances in 1964-66. She has subsequently served as a consultant to Mayor Lindsay's Advisory Panel on Decentralization, an effort aimed at freeing the city's schools from the power hammerlock in which they are held.

In this analysis, Marilyn Gittell has done with the New York City public school system — with clear implications for most large urban school systems — what Lloyd Warner, Robert Havighurst, Robert Dahl, and other social scientists have done with other central structures and institutions of American society. That is, she has held one city's public school system to the light to show where its original basic concepts and ideals have been tarnished or eroded.

The professional educator would be well advised to prepare himself for the future in which the community regains an effective voice in educational policy and decision making. Given such a voice, the public for its part must assume responsibility for preserving and advancing the goals of public education, and it must respect the professional competence of educators. But it also has the right to examine the results of professional efforts, and the main yardstick of performance is the achievement of school children. If the schools are not delivering this product, then the public must have the power to call the process to account and obtain change. Therefore, this book is as much a primer for the educator as it is for the educational reformer. Indeed our best hope is that effective reformers will rise up inside the school system to join those knocking at the gates from without.

Mario D. Fantini
Program Officer, Ford Foundation

Preface

For several decades, educational institutions and educational policy have been insulated from public and expert scrutiny. We know appallingly little about the essential elements of school-policy formulation. While studies of power and decision making proliferate, there has been an apparent reluctance on the part of social scientists to extend such studies to school politics and school politicians. Particularly with regard to large cities, such information is of critical importance if we are to encourage the development of imaginative school policy. The present study of decision making in the New York City school system explores the political forces and the individuals who affect educational policy.

The study was conducted over a three-year period. It was initiated as a consultant's report to New York City's Temporary Commission on City Finances. The later parts of the study were performed pursuant to a contract with the U.S. Department of Health, Education and Welfare, Office of Education, under the provisions of the Cooperative Research Program. I am indebted to both organizations for their financial support.

Research conducted by Shiela Gordon, Rhoda Howard, Cynthia Moten, Beverly Spatt, and Leslie Zolna of the commission staff contributed to the findings. Additional research assistance was provided by Wendy Gismot under a grant from the U.S. Office of Education. And it was through Betty Terrell's exceptional efforts that the final manuscript was typed and submitted in time.

T. E. Hollander, Studies Director for the Education Task Force of the Temporary Commission, played a major role in raising significant questions, discussing key concepts, and exploring the solutions proposed. I would also like to express my appreciation to Allen Rosenthal who provided incisive critical and editorial comment at various stages of the study.

Finally, I would like to thank Harris Dienstfrey for his invaluable editorial assistance.

Table of Contents

Participants and Participation

CHAPTER I

An Approach to Power and Participation

Pluralist concepts of democracy historically have been hinged to a participatory political system. Although modern empirical studies of power have adjusted and redefined some of the unrealistic notions about how a democratic system works, the concept of participation is still used to distinguish open political systems from closed political systems. Almond and Verba, for a typical example, distinguish the democratic state as one that "offers the ordinary man the opportunity to take part in the political decision-making process as an influential citizen."[1] In general, the concept of participation has been refined from one of broad public participation as it is manifested in voting, petitions, and referenda to a stress on the participation of representative leadership through civic and interest-group action. Nevertheless, participation remains the most significant measure of the character and fluidity of a political system.

In technical terms, the two approaches toward studying political behavior in a community — the pluralist and the power elite schools of analysis — disagree on the technique for measuring participation.[2] The pluralists have described power in most larger cities as polylithic, many-sided. Their findings generally identify nonoverlapping, multiple elites. The power elitists have maintained that power structures are predominantly monolithic. These differences have been the cause of a prolonged exchange on methodological approach. But the basic issue, for the purposes of this book, a study of policymaking in the New York City school system, is the general agreement on the matter of participation.

In all of the major studies of decision making in large cities, several areas of policy have been surveyed to substantiate or disprove hypotheses related to the distribution of power. In general, the findings indicate that functional specialization — each area of activity creating its own specialists and professionals — has also resulted in specialization in policymaking. Indeed, looking at the aggregate of city functions, the pluralists have cited the lack of overlap in leadership from one function to another as evidence of a polylithic power structure or a satisfactorily open participatory system. This conclusion is suggested in Dahl's study of New Haven *(Who Governs?)*, Sayre and Kaufman's study of New York City *(Governing New York City)*, and Banfield's study of Chicago *(Political Influence)*.[3] Although each of the studies identified relatively closed decision-making systems in each of the functional areas surveyed, all saw the overall system as open. The assumption implied in the"pluralistic" studies is that although a few men may control decisions in a given functional area, the multiplicity of elite groups over a city-wide basis is the more relevant datum in classifying the political system. For example, Sayre and Kaufman indicate that the central city forces (the mayor and the Board of Estimate) do not really play an integrative role in most areas, yet the authors do not consider that this situation contradicts their overall evaluation of the whole system.[4]

It is clear that functional specialization naturally will produce several distinctive elites within a community, each responsible for policy in a particular area of specialty. Further, if one analyzes more than one function or type of policy, no single group will ever appear to control all of the decisions made in a community. Professionalization and bureaucratic development have assured us of that. But it should also be clear that the only test of the viability of a multiple elite system as a truly participatory political system is the relationship of decision making within a subsystem (or functional area) *to the system as a whole*. Any judgment of the total system must include consideration of the relative openness of various subsystems, their responsiveness to change, and their ability to convert the demands of "clients" into policies.[5] As one student of political research has noted, the pluralists assume that "specialization means that American democracies at the community level are better than they might otherwise be" but they have paid little attention "to the implications of the finding that relatively small numbers of men predominate as active participants over time within a particular domain."[6]

It is quite possible to imagine distinctive patterns of relative openness in certain functional areas, and lack of openness in others. In short, there is no reason to assume that the mere existence of different areas of activity, each with its own group of policymakers, is equivalent to an open political system.

The School as a Political Subsystem

City school systems as political subsystems are worthy of specialized analysis for several reasons. First, school systems are traditionally viewed as arousing more public interest than any other civic activity and, therefore, in principle, should entail a wider base of public participation than other areas of specialization. A lack of wide participation in this area, thus, would be likely to indicate similar or more restricted public activity in other areas of civic concern. In addition, school professionals pride themselves on encouraging public participation in school affairs. Their own ideological underpinnings commit them to public involvement. A study of school policymaking can evaluate how meaningful that ideology has been in achieving participation. Another reason for singling out the school system for analysis is the radical change that has occurred in school populations in large cities over the last two decades. This change has presented a severe challenge to school policymakers and school policy. But perhaps the most immediately important reason for analyzing the area of educational policy is the sheer dearth of information on how school policy is made and who makes it. Educators themselves have been far more concerned with the substance of educational policy and have only recently indicated any interest in the policymaking process. Not to be ignored, finally, is the fact that education represents the largest item of local expenditure and by most standards is the most important local government function.

Until recently, social scientists have virtually ignored the school system as a political institution. The 1954 Supreme Court decision exposed this system to public view and invited studies of desegregation policy. Public involvement and concern was aroused and gradually extended beyond the question of desegregation. As experts began to explore educational policy on school integration, they could not avoid the larger issues of how school systems are organized and how decisions are made.[7] In the last decade there has been an increasing concern with these questions, although published materials are still scarce.

This study of the New York City school system is an effort to describe who participates in school policymaking. Its first purpose is to evaluate the relative openness of the system by describing how school policy is made in several important areas. But it is no less concerned with reassessing Sayre and Kaufman's conclusion that "no single elite dominates the political governmental system of New York." In regard to this second purpose, it carefully examines the school system in terms of Sayre and Kaufman's view that the slow process of change in policy in New York City is due to the government's open channels of access and the city's diversity of interest groups.[8] Hopefully, the type of analysis attempted here has broader implications for the conceptual rationalization of the pluralistic view of power.

CHAPTER II
The Participants

Within any school system, the potential participants in the policymaking process are essentially the same. Legal power is usually divided between a board of education and the superintendent. The bureaucracy breaks down into the central administrative bureaucracy, field administrators, top supervisory staff, and middle management. Organizations representing each of these groups are common in the larger school districts, and the activities of each can be significant. Teachers and teacher organizations, parents and parent organizations, are also potential participants. Specialized education interest groups (ad hoc and permanent) have been active in many communities, and their role can be a vital one. In the general community, there are other potential participants—local, state, and federal officials, civic groups, the press, business organizations, and individual entrepreneurs seeking the rewards of the school system. Interrelationships between these potential participants, the relative power of each, and their role in particular decisions, differs with the nature of the issues and the political environment of the school system.

Participation in school policy formulation can take three forms: (1) *closed* —only the professionals in the system participate; (2) *limited*—the board of education and/or the mayor and specialized educational interest groups participate; and (3) *wide*—groups not wholly concerned with school policy participate.

The Board of Education

The Board of Education in New York City is the official policymaking body for the school system, and its nine members are responsible for long-range educational planning. Traditionally, the appointments of the mayor, who selected the Board until 1961, when his selection was mediated by a civic screening panel, had reflected careful consideration of local interests as well as political favor. The balance of interest was reflected in an implicit religious formula of 3:3:3—three Catholics, three Jews, and three Protestants—and in the appointment of either a Negro or Puerto Rican or both. Geographic distribution demanded by the by-laws assured borough representation. The religious and racial balances, interestingly enough, are continued in the current selection process.[1] (See Table 1.)

TABLE 1

MEMBERS OF BOARD OF EDUCATION:

PERSONAL DATA, 1966

Sex		Age			Religion		
M	F	40-49	50-59	60-69	Protestant	Catholic	Jewish
8	1	2	4	3	3	3	3

There was little question prior to 1961 that the mayor would exercise some measure of control over the Board, and the Board members, in turn, could use their political influence with the mayor. Strong Board presidents who were politically oriented served as the channel for communication with the mayor.[2]

The screening-panel procedure instituted in 1961 strengthened the role of the civic groups and reduced the influence of the mayor. Members of the Board nominated by civic groups are less likely to be intimates of the mayor, and they are less likely to consult with him on school problems. However, people outside the formal school structure, interviewed during this study about the new appointment procedure, expressed dissatisfaction with the lack of political "know-how" of Board members. They pointed out that Board members lack personal influence and no longer can play the political role expected of them by school groups. Of the nine members of the current Board, there are three lawyers, one accountant, one businessman, one labor union official, a civic activist, and two educators. (See Table 2.)

TABLE 2

MEMBERS OF THE BOARD OF EDUCATION:

EDUCATION AND PROFESSIONAL STATUS, 1966

Education levels	
Masters degree	2
Law degree	3
Doctorate	3

Professional Background[a]	
Teacher, lecturer, or professor	6
Labor leader	2
Accountant	1
Attorney	3
Civic organizations in education	1

[a] *Totals are more than 9 because of overlap.*

The Board's role has been largely one of balancing conflicting pressures and interests. Essentially it is a mediator rather than an initiator of policy. As the spokesman for official policy, the Board nominally participates in all major decisions. It spends a great deal of its time, however, on sensitive issues where the balance of power in the Board fails to produce a consensus. These are not necessarily major areas of policy. For example, site-selection controversies have recently occupied an undue amount of Board time. (The Board reviews all questions of site selection when there is disagreement. This is a rather frequent occurrence, particularly since the question of school integration is usually involved.) Other seemingly unimportant but sensitive policy issues have taken up much Board time because the system provides no other way to settle them.

In the five areas selected for examination in the current study — budget, curriculum, selection of superintendent, salary, and integration — the Board's role ranged from superficial participation (in the budget process) to formulation and promulgation of policy — and failure to achieve it (in school integration). On the two major salary increases to emerge in recent years, the Board participated in early negotiations but was satisfied to shift final responsibility to the mayor or his mediators. Selecting a superintendent is the area in which the Board exercised most direct power.

In more general terms, however, the traditional Board had never fulfilled its obligations for long-range planning, and the new Board has not shown any tendency to be more successful in this area than its predecessor. (It seems to be the case that prior to 1961 individual members of the Board were involved in policymaking essentially as a result of their own political stature and their association with the mayor.) In recent years, moreover, the lack of a strong staff has greatly limited the level and character of Board participation. The argument for and against a Board staff has been a continuing one in New York City. Prior to the 1961 upheaval, the Board maintained a strong committee system with a staff assigned to each committee. In 1962, the new Board abandoned this system as an act of good faith to a new superintendent from outside the New York City school system (Calvin Gross). But without staff the Board cannot realistically challenge or review the programs of the administrative bureaucracy, and in 1965 the Board again began to expand its own staff. Nonetheless, as the school system has grown larger and more complex and policies demand more specialized knowledge, the Board has had to withdraw from an effective policy role — a pattern to be seen in several other city school systems.[3] The bureaucracy and special-interest groups have gained power by means of their expertise, while the Board, lacking expertise and political leverage, has lost power.

Local School Boards

In 1961, the Board of Education was empowered to appoint local board members for 25 new district boards.[4] (District selection panels submit two or three names for each vacancy to the district superintendents, who pass the list on to the Board.) The activation of such local school boards was, in part, a recognition of the inadequacy of both one city-wide Board and a system too over-centralized to respond to local needs. The local boards, however, were given no real authority in the determination of school policy. Generally, they have acted as community buffers, holding hearings and discussing narrow local issues, yet they have not had the authority to resolve local problems. Local boards view themselves as preservers of narrow local interests, particularly with regard to integration policy. Officially, the boards rarely act as a body; members are more prone to voice personal views on issues. Local boards do not have the information or facility, much less the authority, to follow through on matters that affect policy.[4a]

The Board of Education has been reluctant to delegate powers to local boards for fear that they would encroach upon its own authority. District superintendents are also hesitant to enhance the position of the local boards for fear that they might interfere with local school administration. As a compromise, the local boards have been assigned the power to hold hearings — which, it seems fair to note, is harmless enough.

Under a 1965 reorganization plan, the 25 districts were increased to 31. The new plan was to promote greater emphasis on decentralized policymaking, utilizing the district superintendent and the local boards more effectively. There is no indication, however, that the plan provides for any basic redistribution of power in the system. Budgeting and personnel policy continue to be centralized, and there is no provision for flexibility in initiating new programs. The present school superintendent has indicated, in an interview, that budgetary procedures in themselves prevent any effective decentralization of the city school system and that policy formulation will remain a headquarters responsibility so long as these procedures are unchanged.

The Superintendent

One of the most confusing aspects of school administration in New York City has been the growth in power of the administrative staff while the superintendent has remained a relatively limited chief executive. In part, it is the very strength of the bureaucracy that has undermined the role of the superintendent.[5]

Nine superintendents have served the city school system since 1898. (See Table 3.) As the table shows, the first superintendent's tenure was the longest, a period of 20 years. The other eight superintendents have had notably shorter terms of office. The two superintendents preceding the present incumbent (Bernard Donovan) served respectively four- and three-year terms. The relatively short tenure in office of the last four superintendents has undoubtedly taken its toll so far as the power of the office is concerned. (The high casualty rate of superintendents appears to be characteristic of several large cities.[6]) Open conflict between the superintendent and the Board was evidenced in three of the last four administrations, one such conflict resulting in the superintendent's dismissal.[7] Although over the long run the Board has lost power vis-à-vis the bureaucracy and special-interest groups, vis-à-vis the superintendent, it still remains the more powerful. The last two Board presidents have

TABLE 3

SUPERINTENDENTS OF SCHOOLS IN NEW YORK CITY,
1898-1965

Name	Date	Years of Office
William H. Maxwell	1898-1918	20
William L. Ettinger	1918-1928	6
William J. O'Shea	1928-1934	10
Harold G. Campbell	1934-1942	8
John E. Wade	1942-1947	5
William Jansen	1947-1958	11
John Theobald	1958-1962	4
Calvin Gross[a]	1962-1965	3
Bernard Donovan	1965-	

[a] *The only superintendent who had no previous experience in the New York City school system.*

proudly claimed that they devoted at least 45 hours a week to their jobs, indicating both a day-to-day involvement in school affairs that in all probability ought to be left to the superintendent and a general lack of reliance on the superintendent for policy recommendations.

Individual superintendents vary in the degree to which they exercise the powers of the office. Such differences can be measured in terms of their relationship to the Board and to the supervisory staff, and in their rapport with public-interest groups.

But despite such variance, there are important structural limitations to the superintendent's executive powers. The superintendent in New York City lacks the most essential power of a strong executive, the power of appointment and removal. The system's supervisory staff is developed completely through promotion from the ranks. Tenured supervisors hold top policymaking jobs, allowing the superintendent little flexibility in appointments. All assistant superintendents receive tenure after a three-year probationary period. The ingrown quality of the staff was increased by the last previous superintendent (Gross), who further encumbered his own appointive powers by establishing a procedure under which the existing assistant superintendents provided him with a list of recommended candidates for the selection of future assistant superintendents. While the list has no official status, any deviation from its recommendations would most assuredly incur the wrath of the group that had drawn it up. The superintendent is further debilitated by his dependency on the Board of Examiners. It is not uncommon for the Examiners to delay examination and approval of candidates for assistant superintendent whom the superintendent may wish to appoint to his own staff.

The effect of all this is that no superintendent can rely on his own team of trusted advisors. He cannot freely develop his own advisory staff and is encumbered by the appointments and promotions made by his predecessors. Appointments from outside the system are almost nonexistent. (It appears that any superintendent from outside the system, and not himself subject to its loyalties, is likely to find his task all the more difficult. The only such superintendent in New York history is Calvin Gross, who occupied the office from 1962-65. A magazine article, written after his dismissal, correctly noted that "Gross could have made a real dent on the New York City schools if only he had had a handful of trusted special assistants."[8])

Loyalties developed within such an environment are strong and are based largely on who appointed whom. Top level deputy and assistant superintendents have moved up in the separate divisions of the system, and their loyal-

ties are based on their associations in these divisions. Some individuals undoubtedly think they should have been superintendent. This results in much
backbiting and petty jealousies.

The superintendent thus must cope with the potentially competing interests
of his own supervisory bureaucracy.[9] Further, on occasion, directives and policy
statements issued by the superintendent on key policies have been attacked
by his own supervisory staff, both by the staff's professional organizations
and, officially, through the organized committees on which the staff members
sit.

In March of 1964, the Council of Supervisory Associations — a professional
organization made up of the various supervisory associations — issued a general statement condemning policies of the then superintendent (Gross) and
noting his failure to consult with his professional staff before making decisions.
In a more recent controversy the High School Principals Association criticized
the incumbent superintendent (Donovan) for interfering with a principal's
decision on school dress regulation.[10]

In the area of the budget, the superintendents' lack of power is also notable.
Several days spent in the budget office at headquarters indicated that the budget office staff did not act in either a policymaking or an advisory capacity.
Budget estimates are based essentially on preestablished ratios of books and
teachers to pupils, with slight adjustments according to the type of school.
Budget approvals come from division heads and are reviewed in hearings controlled by the same people. In short, the budget-making process is quite outside the control of the superintendent. (This is discussed more fully in the
next chapter.) The last previous superintendent met with his budget director
only *once* a year.

The procedures and influences in the choice of the superintendent pre-
condition his ability to control the system he must direct. His choice is so much
dependent upon his ability to rise within that system that he can hardly be expected to challenge it once he takes office. His own rise to power is an indication of his acceptance of established interests and loyalties; his success as superintendent is a further measure of his willingness to support and enhance those
interests.

The Bureaucracy

The education bureaucracy in New York City must be viewed in at least
two separate categories: (1) the headquarters staff and (2) the operational field

staff. A precise figure on the size of the headquarters staff is difficult to determine; it is estimated to be somewhere around 3,000. At least four-to-five-hundred people working at headquarters do not appear in its budget. Although serving as full-time headquarters personnel, they are paid out of local school budgets. The operational field staff includes some 2,200 principals and assistant principals, 31 district superintendents, and 740 department chairmen. (See Appendix A.)

A core supervisory group which holds much of the decision-making power includes some 30 headquarters staff members — including the executive deputy superintendent and the deputy superintendent in charge of instruction and curriculum, the Board of Examiners, 20 of the 30 assistant superintendents, and a few active directors of special bureaus. Much of the power which has been lodged in this central staff has prevented the expansion of the role of the district superintendents, who function in a liaison capacity and who although nominally supervisory, practically speaking are an anachronism in the system.

With the exception of two assistant superintendents, who had experience in school systems outside of New York City, the entire core supervisory group was bred within the New York City school system — many as principals, almost all with long experience at headquarters. A review of the background of the 26 top supervisory staff members revealed that their careers followed a general pattern. Having served as principals or assistant principals, they were brought into the Board on special assignment and/or had served on special committees (usually as a result of contacts already established at headquarters). (See Tables 4, 5, and 6.)

Although no extensive analysis of the ethnic and religious backgrounds of supervisors was attempted, it was evident that the supervisors were predominantly Catholic and Jewish. The more recent appointments include a larger proportion of Jews, while the highest ranking positions are held by Catholics. In 1965 the three top ranking officials were Catholic. There are very few Negroes in supervisory positions at headquarters and a limited number of Negro school principals throughout the city. Assignment to headquarters staff by school division reinforces the loyalties of staff members to that division and its supervisory staff. In all school reorganization proposals, these loyalties have repeatedly fostered preservation of the *status quo*.

TABLE 4

ASSISTANT SUPERINTENDENTS, HEADQUARTERS
(Sample of 26)

Highest Graduate Degree Held, 1966	
None	2
Masters	16
Law	2[a]
Doctorate	8

[a] *Two superintendents held a law and a masters degree.*

TABLE 5

ASSISTANT SUPERINTENDENTS, HEADQUARTERS
(Sample of 26)

Age, 1966 [a]	
40-50	2
51-60	13
61-70	11

[a] *Some ages represent estimates based on biographical data.*

TABLE 6

ASSISTANT SUPERINTENDENTS, FIELD
(Sample of 26)

Years in Present Position		Years in NYC School System [a]			
0-5	6-10	10-20	21-30	31-40	41-50
20	6	1	6	14	5

[a] *Some figures are estimates based on biographical data.*

In almost every area of school policy it was evident that those at headquarters, particularly the core of 30-odd supervisors, were major policymakers. They exercise power individually as heads of divisions and departments, and as a group they act to reinforce their individual decisions. Overcentralization has long plagued the New York City school system, and several studies have stressed the need for thorough administrative reorganization.[11] Yet it seems clear that the Board's efforts along these lines, led by the last two superintendents, have been thwarted by the vested interests of the staff in maintaining the *status quo.*[12]

District Superintendents

The supervisors in the field are the district superintendents. These men represent the only means by which the present structure can achieve any administrative decentralization and the system's only source of professional liaison with local school needs. A detailed questioning of nine of the 25 district superintendents indicated that the superintendents do not participate in the formulation of school policy. Most of the individuals interviewed complained that they were not involved significantly in budgeting, curriculum implementation, assignment of personnel, or formulation of general school policy. Very few had meaningful relations with headquarters staff. Their contact with schools was limited to periodic visits and to meetings with principals, but rarely with teachers. The superintendents believed that even if they could pinpoint special local needs, there was not much that they could do about dealing with them. (See Appendix B.) In part, then, the ineffectiveness of the superintendents is due to their own narrow understanding of their function.

But it is also due to their general lack of budgetary and personnel powers. District superintendents have no discretion in the distribution of funds and only the most limited kind of discretion in the assignment of personnel. Their staffs are small and largely clerical. In practical terms, district superintendents act as a buffer for parent dissatisfaction that remains unresolved by the school principal. The superintendents' lack of participation in policy decisions gives support to the central conclusion of this study, that the central supervisory staff has cornered the power market.[13]

Supervisory Associations

As already noted, the Council of Supervisory Associations, organized in 1962, is a professional organization made up of the various individual supervisory associations — including those for high school principals, junior high school principals, elementary school principals, assistant principals, high school chairmen, the Board of Examiners, assistant superintendents, and associate superintendents. Invariably, policies which require fundamental institutional change are challenged by the supervisory staff through the Council, which has close to 3,000 members. Through the individual associations, and jointly through the Council, even though it has no formal position in the school system, the vested interests of the supervisory staff exert a strong influence in education policy.[14] The Council has openly opposed the Princeton Plan, school busing, the comprehensive high school plan, the dropping of I.Q. examinations, and school pairing —*after* they were adopted as official policy by the Board and by the superintendent.[15] It is noteworthy that with one exception (dropping the I.Q. examinations) none of these policies was implemented.

The Teachers and the Union

Because of the power it wields in collective bargaining, the United Federation of Teachers is among the system's major policymakers. The Union, whose membership in New York City is over 30,000, is the official bargaining agent for the city's teachers. The Union contract determines wide areas of personnel practices, expenditures, and teaching allotments. Because salaries and teachers' benefits represent close to half the total education budget, the Union is directly involved in matters of finance. The potential power of the Union to participate in other policy areas has not been fully realized because of its own decision to concentrate its attention on salary scales and related benefits. The teachers as a group do not participate, for example, in the most obvious area in which their expertise would be extremely helpful, the development of curriculum. (With the exception of a few high school specialists, the Bureau of Curriculum Research, for its part, has made no effort to involve teachers in its programs.) Nor is there any evidence to indicate that teachers were consulted on integration policy or about the problems of ghetto schools. Teachers are not at all involved in budgeting or selection of the superintendent, either through the Union or as individuals.[16]

In sum, the Union can be viewed as representing another large "professional" group engaged in policymaking in education that functions as a satellite rather than as a core group. Its membership comprises the largest group of professionals in the school system. In the few limited areas (outside of salary policy and related fringe benefits) on which it has taken a public position, it appears to have been motivated largely by a desire to maintain the *status quo*. The Union has publicly and privately fought transfers of experienced teachers to difficult schools, and the rotation plan has reamined a voluntary program. It has also questioned the advisability of a 4:4:4 school reorganization because the plan threatened the status of the junior high school teacher. On the other hand, it has advanced the More Effective Schools proposal, that called for the creation of several specially staffed schools with low pupil-teacher ratios. From interviews conducted with Union leaders, it was clear that they themselves saw a conflict between, on the one hand, educational and professional goals, and, on the other, the narrow interests of its membership. In some instances the Union leaders expressed concern that their own positions of power might be threatened if they violated the narrower interests of their membership.

Local Civic and Interest Groups

It should be clear from this description that education decision making is closely circumscribed within the functional specialization of the New York City political system. However, the professional school bureaucracy is answerable in some circumstances to an organized clientele that reflects the same kind of specialization. Specifically, two interest groups in New York City share the responsibility for overseeing education policy: the United Parents Association and the Public Education Association. Board membership in both organizations overlap, and the two professional staffs work closely together.

The United Parents Association is a central city-wide organization made up of delegates elected by local school-parent associations that have chosen to join the central city agency. The Parents Association is generally reformist in orientation, although it is highly selective in its campaigns. Its leadership has been drawn largely from the Jewish community.[17] Its general membership is drawn largely from middle-class white parents, who are primarily concerned with local school problems and facilities. The Association accordingly has directed much of its attention to these issues. In recent years, site selection controversies and school integration problems have occupied much of its time.

The Association speaks for parents and maintains a direct concern with the immediate effects of policy on local school situations. It has at times taken general policy positions on "key" issues and when possible makes use of direct influence with Board of Education members. A current member of the Board was an officer of the Association prior to her appointment and still maintains active communication with it. The Association's executive director was recently appointed a staff advisor to the Board. The Association has supported the appointment of supervisory staff in the Board of Education and appears to have viable contacts within the bureaucracy. Although it is unlikely that the Association could stimulate city-wide support for certain policies, it has effectively used this threat to influence staff and Board decisions. By and large, however, the Association supports current school policy and offers little in the way of alternatives.

The Public Education Association is a composite group representing professional education interests in the city that are outside of the school system itself. Board members of the PEA represent the major civic groups in the city. The Association's activities have centered on the long-range educational aspects of school policy. Its strategy has been to study special problems and to make public recommendations based on its studies. One of the Association's reports contributed significantly to rethinking and reshaping school policy on vocational schools.[18] In general, the views of the United Parents Association and Public Education Association on any issue are never far apart, although the latter has tended to support greater independence for the school system in all areas, while the former seems to prefer continued reliance on financial support from the city.

Since 1961, the screening-panel method of selecting the Board of Education has given the two Associations a more direct role in the selection of Board members. Both groups are represented on the panel and exercise a notable influence in the nomination process.

As will be seen, the Public Education Association has directly attempted to influence the selection of the last four superintendents. An increase in its influence became apparent when the new Board was instituted in 1961. Prior to that time, the Association had not been successful in its efforts to bring in an outsider as superintendent, and its recommendations had been virtually ignored. It has been an important influence, however, in the last two appointments.

On the whole, the role of both Associations as overseers of educational policy is supportive rather than critical. Their inclination is to work within the structure, focusing on particular problems. Neither has suggested any radical change. Both groups exercise little influence in the area of curriculum. On occasion, one, or both, have made general statements regarding the need for the inclusion of certain material in the curriculum, or for greater emphasis in a given field, but such concern is sporadic and unfocused. Both have supported increased school expenditures and larger city and state appropriations.

The Press

Education reporting in the New York City press is rather limited. *The New York Times* has an education editor (currently, Fred Hechinger), but his weekly and sparse columns are concerned largely with national education matters. Periodically, local school issues that have implication for other school systems are covered. A regular *Times* education reporter (Leonard Buder) is more intimately concerned with local matters. His column appears several times a week, except of course when there is a controversy worthy of a daily news story. School desegregation controversies receive a great deal of attention. Buder's constant attention to school affairs serves the purpose of providing a select group of *Times'* readers with information that might otherwise be hidden. He has not, however, delved into school problems independently. The paper's editorials on education are generally supportive of the school system and mild in their approach.

The only recent critical article on the school system was as a part of a series on the "City In Crisis" in the now defunct *Herald Tribune.* Its focus was primarily on the schools' lack of adequate resources.[19]

Joseph Pois, in his study of a school board crisis in Chicago, notes that newspaper scrutiny has had a very important impact on the board operations in that city. He implies that reporting on the board's position and the votes within it touches sensitive areas of concern.[20] Reporting in New York papers is not so probing.

CHAPTER III

The Educational Environment

A Changing Population

The school system is the city in microcosm. Its problems are the problems of a metropolis, its current needs a reflection of the increasing pressures of a changing population. The ability of the system to adapt to such changes is integral to its success or failure. Much depends upon the responsiveness of those with power and their ability to develop policies appropriate to the task. No small part of the task is the sheer magnitude of its context. The size and political complexity of large cities cannot be overestimated as an important aspect of the problem of educational change.

In New York City, the total school register increased 16 per cent[1] during the last decade. In itself, the increase is not substantial. What is important is the radical change in the composition of the school population.

The critical factor in the change has been the loss of over 800,000 of the city's middle-class whites and the influx of 700,000 Puerto Ricans and Negroes. Between 1957-58 and 1964-65, while the number of Negro and Puerto Rican pupils in the public schools increased by 64 and 46 per cent respectively, the number of white (other) pupils decreased by 13 per cent.[2] Negro and Puerto Rican children comprised over 45 per cent of the school population in 1964-65, compared with 32 per cent in 1957-58. Population forecasts indicate that no matter what policies are adopted for the public schools, the proportion of Negro and Puerto Rican pupils will exceed 66 per cent in 1970 and 70 per cent in 1975.[3]

A high proportion of these children do and will come from homes where the problems associated with poverty overshadow all others. Thus, the city's schools must recognize and cope with the consequences in their students of family instability, low educational level of parents, lack of parental supervision, poor housing, and poor health. The schools must also overcome basic educational handicaps common to such young people, including poor speech and language problems, fewer indirect learning experiences, fewer opportunities for solving problems, and less interaction between adults and children.[4]

The problems for the schools have been aggravated further by the shift of white middle-class students from public to private schools and by the concentration of the Negro and Puerto Rican population in certain sections of the city, and especially in certain boroughs. Manhattan is most affected; its school population is now over 70 per cent Negro and Puerto Rican.[5] (See Table I, Appendix A.)

Coping with a school population that has changed so rapidly requires, first of all, immense efforts by those responsible for educational policy and, secondly, large changes in the school system itself.

Demands and Needs

The New York City school system has been the beneficiary of substantial increases in funds and personnel over the last decade with seemingly little effective change in the calibre of the system as a whole and with only limited success in special programs.

There has been, for one thing, a substantial growth in the number of teachers. While from 1954 to 1964 pupil enrollment rose 16 per cent, the increase of educational employees was double that, or 37 per cent. (See Table IV, Appendix A.) At the elementary school level, the number of instructional positions increased by 24 per cent, while enrollment rose only 4.5 per cent. In particular, the number of guidance, remedial reading, library, and other special service teachers grew sizably.[6]

However, despite the large and generally disproportionate (to enrollment) increases in instructional staff, *there has been little change in class size.* The majority of classes in New York City schools have had and continue to have 30 or more pupils. The "improvement" in pupil-teacher ratio has come about through an increase in teaching positions *outside* the classroom.

For example, of the 2,500 new teachers added to the elementary school staff in the past ten years, 1,000 teach the teachers — that is, they provide one preparation period a week for regular classroom teachers. Further, 100 of the new "service teachers" do not teach at all, but are assigned to field superintendents' offices as coordinators of reading, science, mathematics, or health.

Many of the new special service teachers have been included in new programs geared toward educationally backward children. The host of such new programs, includes Higher Horizons, after school study centers, corrective reading programs, reading clinics, the new summer elementary school programs, prekindergarten programs, early identification and prevention programs, junior guidance and career guidance programs. While each program takes a slightly different tack (e.g., corrective reading is for retarded readers, while the reading clinic is for children whose reading ability appears hampered by emotional problems), all of them are based on the premise that compensatory and complementary services will bring to the "culturally deprived" child the advantages enjoyed by his "culturally privileged" counterpart.

Although a listing of these programs is impressive, the results have been far from successful. Where evaluations have been made, as in the case of the Higher Horizons program, there have been very few notable results.[7] In other cases, the programs represent more narrowly conveived experiments affecting only a small number of students. The basic point is this, that no *fundamental* changes in the school system have been made to meet the vast changes in the city's population. The issue can be put even more strongly: The New York City school system has appeared paralyzed in the face of the massive school problems of the postwar years. Despite its series of compensatory programs, it has shown itself unable to adapt or innovate adequately to stem a precipitous downhill trend. Large, cumbersome, and burdened by a congested bureaucracy, the school system has suffered from inertia or has responded dilatorily to the new major demands being made on it.

The personnel of the system are variously aware of its failures, and different groups ascribe the blame to different sources. While the administrators in the system berate poor teaching, the teachers are critical of the supervisory staff; and the Board of Education divides responsibility between the two. Certainly, the selection of highly qualified personnel on every level would add considerably to the system. A recent profile of a school principal in a Manhattan ghetto school suggests the contribution that can be made by thoughtul, creative, and talented people within the system.[8] However, the procedures for selection of personnel, the standards for maintaining or enhancing one's position, and the environment in which one functions are all a product of the total complex of the system's decision-making structure.

For example, while several major studies over the past dozen years have called for drastic changes in the Board of Examiners in order to improve and facilitate the selection of teachers and promotions to administrative ranks, the Board of Examiners has remained solidly intact. Further, while the Preusse (1959) and other major studies have called for reorganization of the school system, only in 1965 was a plan *offered,* and procedures for implementation of that plan have not been forthcoming. And while study after study (Strayer-Yavner, 1951; Preusse, 1959; Heald, 1959; Schinnerer, 1961; Gulick, 1963) has called for a clear differentiation between the duties of the Board of Education and the superintendent, the line is still unclear and the position of the superintendent of schools is still relatively weak.[9] Significantly, while the Board of Education initially set out a strong program for integration, delay and indecision hamstrung the program and debilitated it. In effect, the problems are known, but very little is done.

Any indictment of the city school system can be fortified with an array of evidence that illustrates deficiencies in teaching, administration, school plant, and most significantly, the performance of students. More than half the city's pupils are behind the national norms of their grade level. In two series of tests given to the city's school children, results showed that 53.9 per cent of the second graders were below national norms in reading, as were three-fifths of the pupils in the fourth grade. In the administration of the Iowa Achievement tests, 54.5 per cent of the fourth graders and 58.6 per cent of the sixth graders were below national norms. In arithmetic, 59.8 per cent of the fourth graders scored below national norms, as did 60.6 per cent of the sixth graders.[10] This evidence in and of itself is indicative of the failure of New York City's school system. Such conditions as the obsolete school plants, lack of adequate textbooks, and outdated facilities could also be cited.[11]

A persistent lack of fundamental change in basic components of the educational system is the most incriminating evidence. New York City has not witnessed any meaningful change in curriculum, administrative structure, teaching recruitment, appointment and training, or general organization for at least three decades. The source of educational policy, how and by whom decisions are made, therefore is a matter of vital concern.

Educational policy encompasses all of the decisions related to the operation of the school system. To determine how policy is made and the relative power of the various participants to influence decisions, this analysis focused on a cross section of school policy. The selection was based on the need to include different types of policy, while allowing for the widest possible variation in the degrees of participation and kinds of participants. Policy was viewed not as a matter of single decisions but in the context of a continuum — as a series of decisions of the same kind made over a period of time.

Five areas were selected for intensive study: (1) appointment of the superintendent; (2) increases in teachers' salaries; (3) budgeting; (4) school integration; and (5) curriculum development.[12]

Over a period of a year and a half, all newspaper items in two daily newspapers were analyzed, with the object of recording all public statements and reports on education policy. These items were categorized by participant and issue, providing a general picture of the public roles and concerns of all participants. A series of detailed, selective interviews with Board of Education members and their professional staff were then conducted. Findings were cross-checked in interviews with participants outside the school system, including staff members of the Public Education Association, United Federation of Teachers, and other civic groups. Lawyers and educators, knowledgeable in school affairs, were also consulted. A special survey questionnaire was developed for longer interviews with half the field superintendents in the system. The files of civic groups were researched for relevant data on specific issues. Finally, a search was made of all professional and popular literature for accounts of decision making in other school systems for comparative purposes.

CHAPTER IV

Professionals Decide: The Monopolization of Budgeting and Curriculum Policy

Lack of innovation and continued reliance on past programs and practices is especially notable in two major areas of school policy, curriculum development and budgeting. Both of these areas of policy are so completely controlled by the supervisory bureaucracy at headquarters that even satellite groups with special interests in such matters have been removed from policy decisions. Thus, these two areas provide examples of *closed* participation — functional specialization in more or less pure form.

School Budgeting

Budgeting policy can be a major instrument for developing a continuous evaluation of and innovation within a system, or it can be a bookkeeping operation supporting the *status quo*. Developments on the federal level indicate the potential of budget review as a source of alternative policy formulation. Comprehensive program planning and review combined with budget analysis is spreading from the Defense Department to other agencies in the federal government. These new techniques, which rely on the most up-to-date technological developments, offer the means for more broadly conceived policymaking.

The implications of budget policy are so enormous that they reflect on all other aspects of educational policy. The Board of Education, in contrast to other city departments, has wide discretion. It is the only city agency with a "lump-sum" appropriation rather than the usual "line-item" appropriation, thereby effectively giving it complete control over its expense budget.

The Board has received a lump-sum appropriation since 1962.[1] A 1963 memorandum of understanding, signed by the mayor, the comptroller, and the president of the Board of Education, spells out the freedom of the Board to allocate and administer its funds. The Board can shift funds from one program to another without specific approval of the mayor, the Board of Estimate, or the Bureau of the Budget, though in certain instances it must hold public hearings. The Board needs the approval of the mayor only for increases in the *total* budget allotment.[2] Further, the Board's control of its budget is essentially free from state control.[3]

The only non-Board personnel who participate in the budget process are the two budget examiners assigned to the Board of Education by the city's budget director. In June or July each year, the examiners submit a five-year budget estimate to the director. The estimate is based on conversations with operating division administrators; on a review of current programs, new programs, class size, pupil register; and on projections of the data developed from this review. In September, the examiners meet with the headquarters staff to discuss the budget for the coming fiscal year on the basis of revised pupil registers and other changes that may have taken place. Although the examiners are directed to make field visits, ostensibly to determine whether utilization of facilities is in line with the figures cited in the justification of the current year's budget, they have little time for that kind of activity.

The examiners' only job is to provide the mayor and budget director with estimates of the funds needed to continue existing programs. Their estimates are taken from the Board's own staff. Their function is purely one of liaison, and they are not in any way involved in school programing or the determination of budget policy.

Though the Board has extensive control over its area of concern, its budget making, as with most units of government, is incremental, fragmented, and nonprogrammatic. Determination of the size and content of a given year's budget is based on the previous year's budget, with allowances for increased costs of equipment, supplies, scheduled salary increments, and increased rates of pay.

There is very little flexibility in the budget because of the tremendous number of commitments that are made years in advance. It has been estimated that mandated expenditures make up to 60 per cent of the budget. Most items are automatically approved year after year.

An important part of budgeting policy is the establishment of standards for the entire school system. The only standard established by law (in the bylaws of the Board) is the ratio of assistant principals and administrative assistants to teachers. Otherwise, determinations of average class size, teacher-student ratio, the ratio of clerks to pupils, the per capita allotment for textbooks and supplies, and the allocation of librarians and other teaching positions are made each year.

Allocations of books and supplies are made in November for the coming fiscal year, based on the amount of money that had been available for this pur-pose during the previous year. This allocation is then broken down into a per capita amount for each of the three categories of schools in the system — spe-cial service, more effective, and regular.[4] The differential is decided upon by the superintendent in charge of each operating division.[5] Withheld from this allocation is an amount estimated for reserves in case there should be a cut-back, a new program, or an unforeseen contingency.

In addition, the bureaus of Home Economics, Industrial Arts, Health Edu-cation, and CRMD services, and other special bureaus get lump-sum amounts that they in turn allocate to the schools, also on the basis of the number of special classes and the number of students.

Local boards and district superintendents have little or no discretion in the development of the budget. Adjustments to local needs are nonexistent (ex-cept in formulas established for special service category schools). Individual principals have no budget leeway; they are restricted by headquarters policies and directives. (Each district superintendent and principal has a small fund to meet special costs.) A result of this procedure is that experimentation or new programs are possible only as they are developed at headquarters and given budget confirmation.

Budgeting, in short, is a central operation, developed at school headquarters and controlled by the core supervisory staff. The supervisory staff's discus-sions, held from the middle of August to the middle of September, define budgeting objectives and govern preparation of budget requests by the various divisions and bureaus. In late September, each division submits its formal budget requests to the school system's Office of Business Affairs. Justification for requests is outlined in the forms that accompany submissions. Each super-intendent who heads a division at headquarters reviews requests under his jurisdiction prior to their submission and again in hearings after submission. The compilation prepared by the Office of Business Affairs is submitted to the superintendent of schools in early November and then to the Board of Education. Public hearings are held by the Board at the end of December, and the budget is adopted by December 30.

Final acceptance must await the presentation of the entire city budget by the mayor to the Board of Estimate and the City Council in the following April. Public hearings are scheduled when the mayor presents his budget to the Board of Estimate. After the mayor's budget is prepared with a lump-sum appropria-tion for education, the Board of Education must adjust its line-item schedule to the lump-sum appropriation made by the city. Usually this is done within a week to meet the scheduled hearings on the city budget. Final adoption of the city budget may not be until as late as the middle of June.[6]

These procedures and the time schedule suggest the pressures on budgeting policy that make the process more a matter of routine than intensive analysis. Because of the limited amount of time between the mayor's lump-sum budget appropriation and the hearings before the City Council and the Board of Estimate, citizens' groups have little opportunity to study the budget or offer alternatives. Their influence on budget policy is, therefore, severely restricted. The Board of Education itself has inadequate staff and time to carefully review the budget. Also, the lack of program analysis impedes the Board's ability to contribute significantly to budget policy. One of the Board members, a certified public accountant, in his attempts to review the school budget, has commented on the lack of information available to the Board.[7] Each new budget focuses the Board's attention only on a narrow range of increases and decreases from the previous year. The budget document is never reviewed as a whole, in the sense of re-evaluating existing programs and activities.

Policy changes can be made after the budget has been adopted. Under current modification procedures, the Board of Education can transfer large sums of money without prior public notice or hearing. It must report to the public only on transfers between seven major program categories. In defining its programs, the Board has drawn them so broadly that almost every concern is included under the two programs titled "Curriculum Research and Evaluation" and "Instruction." Included under "Instruction" are the various school operating divisions as well as Recreation, the Bureau of Child Guidance, Early Childhood Education, and the Bureau of Vocational and Educational Guidance. The budget for Instruction covers $578 million or two-thirds of the total funds administered by the Board. Millions of dollars, therefore, could be transferred from elementary to junior high schools without any public notice.

More important, policy formally adopted by the Board could be changed through a process of staff modification. Thus, the transfer of teachers to other than teaching assignments can result in an increase in class size despite the fact that the justification for creating additional positions may have been to reduce class size.

The Office of Business Affairs at headquarters maintains strict control over budget policy. An interview with the current director of Business Affairs made it clear that he saw no need to provide more information on the budget to the public or outside groups. The office is currently programming I.B.M. equipment for budgeting and financial purposes and, once this is completed, the factor of prohibitive costs could alone be used as an argument against changes in procedures. (Local civic groups recently have indicated their concern that budget policy will be even more internalized at headquarters in the future. Their concern is based in part on the fact that in 1965-66 there was only a four day period between the publication of the budget in September and the first public hearings.)

The importance of the budget as a plan for school programs and policy cannot be underestimated. New programs never see the light of day if they do not have the support of the superintendents in charge of the special divisions. The four or five headquarters superintendents who review budget requests are the first and final authority in the translation of programs to budget policy. This tightly-structured procedure establishes inflexible standards for 80 to 90 per cent of the budget. The central budgeting staff establishes standards for the entire school system, tieing the hands of the local school administrators and undermining their ability to respond to individual needs. The staff uses none of the existent methods for advanced program planning and evaluation, thus greatly restricting the consideration of policy alternatives. Public discussion of the budget is virtually impossible, and civic and interest-group participation is severely limited. Even the Board and the superintendent of schools are chained to a document that may have little to do with their hopes or intentions. At present, the budget cannot be viewed in any way as a tool of the superintendent, and it is even less a statement of the Board of Education's policy.[8]

Curriculum Policy

Analyzing participation in curriculum decisions can be distorted by the particular issue on which one focuses. If one reviews the adoption of a single change, such as the introduction of Negro history, interest-group influences (particularly civil rights groups) and Board pressure are evident. Certainly in the case of recent curriculum changes in mathematics and science, the national scientific community has indirectly influenced revisions. The introduction of such changes, however, does not touch on the basic design of the curriculum as a whole. Curriculum is defined by educators as organizationally planned and controlled experiences designed to educate students. It involves content and process. Curriculum development is the political process by which choices are made for changing educational institutions.[9] It is this process that was selected for analysis.

The deputy superintendent in charge of curriculum and instruction in New

York City is administratively responsible for the coordination of curriculum development and implementation. In that capacity he is a major influence in planning curriculum programs and in the initiation of curriculum research projects. Until recently, research and evaluation were entirely distinctive tasks, separate in turn from curriculum development. The former deputy superintendent indicated the need to tighten control over these operations. Prior to 1965, a curriculum council, composed of key headquarter supervisors, met regularly to discuss and initiate curriculum research. This function is now performed by the deputy superintendent and his small personal cabinet. Several curriculum specialists who were interviewed indicated that the initiation of new projects was now completely in the hands of the deputy superintendent. They suggested that the curriculum experts (referring to themselves) were not consulted on matters they thought they should be involved in, and they characterized the situation as a conflict between administrative and professional interests, with administrative interests dominating.

The Bureau of Curriculum Research, a headquarters operation, is the officially designated school agency for the development of curriculum. It has a professional staff with the equivalent of 27 full-time positions, that function under the aegis of an assistant superintendent. The bureau itself functions under the deputy superintendent. Many of the decisions that are naturally involved in the preparation of curriculum bulletins are routinized by procedures in the bureau.

For example, the bureau reviews and rewrites all curriculum bulletins. The bulletins provide guidelines for the school curriculum in each subject area. All bulletins are reviewed within a three-to-five-year period. At the beginning of each year the bureau staff reviews bulletins which are three-to-five-years old and selects those to be revised. The object is "to keep new things coming out." In some instances, the decision to revise is in response to a recommendation of the deputy superintendent.

In several fields the department chairmen's committees in the high schools have encouraged curriculum revision. As subject matter specialists, they maintain an active interest in their fields and are, therefore, more concerned with the content of the curriculum. They are the only group of teachers noticeably involved in curriculum policy. Junior high school teachers participate in curriculum revisions only in rare instances. Elementary school people are almost never involved. Although the bureau routinely sends out questionnaires to solicit opinions from teachers, staff members have indicated that the response is not generally significant.

When it is determined that a bulletin is to be revised, a committee — comprised mainly of central staff members from the bureau and other headquarters divisions — is appointed and assigned the task. Few teachers are included on the committees, and there is very limited use of consultants outside of the school system. The school people utilized are usually administrative personnel, principals, and assistant principals. In an interview the head of the Bureau stated that he encouraged the assignment of teachers, but there was always too much difficulty getting them transferred to temporary assignments to work on a particular project. Getting teachers released for such assignments requires the approval of headquarters and arranging for a replacement. Budget increases are also required to pay for additional personnel Transferring staff within headquarters is much easier to accomplish, and there are no financial problems because personnel can be transferred from one headquarters department to another.

Essentially, then, the development of curriculum — which amounts to the preparation and revision of curriculum bulletins — is a headquarters job, removed from schools, teachers, and the most expert thinking in the field. Although curriculum theory stresses flexibility and innovation, the procedures for the development of curriculum in New York City are constrained by the bureaucratic structure. Fundamental innovation is not a likely outgrowth of such a system, and in fact over the years changes have been narrowly conceived. Although radical shifts in the school population should have stimulated broad revisions in curriculum, no such revisions have been made, and given the usual procedures, none is likely. As a case in point, in developing a new curriculum for an extensive preschool program, the committee was expected to come up with a plan in two to three weeks.

Once a curriculum program has been developed, curriculum coordinators supervise its implementation. The coordinators perform two main duties: they coordinate the work of local district curriculum assistants, and they provide a liaison between the Bureau of Curriculum Research and the school divisions. Particular headquarters bureaus (e.g., Bureau of Science) also assign subject-area coordinators in special fields to the districts.

Each local school district maintains a curriculum committee that is composed of the curriculum coordinator, representatives of the superintendent's office, and principals and teachers of the district. The ostensible function of the committees is to review local needs.

Curriculum assistants are chosen by district superintendents (one for each district) on the recommendation of principals. Usually these are people from within the districts. The assistants spend 60 per cent of their time in the field and the remaining time at the bureau office. Meetings are held weekly with the curriculum coordinator. Curriculum specialists rarely engage in discussions with the teaching staff. They meet with principals in the district and rely upon them to translate the new curriculum programs to their teaching staff. The specialists' guidelines are the curriculum bulletins. The practices and procedures employed by principals to implement curriculum policy as it is promulgated in the bulletins of the bureau vary from school to school, but are usually less than adequate. Most principals have little time to develop programs for introducing new curriculum to teachers. In some cases, the principal's limited ability in such matters prevents a meaningful follow-through. Finally, time restrictions for teachers' meetings (under the current union contract) make communication or discussions on these questions difficult to arrange.

Implementation of curriculum is a complex matter, to say the least. In the final analysis, teachers and principals are the determinants of what is taught in the classroom. Curriculum experts have ascertained, however, that as a rule the classroom teacher rarely is an innovator, so that the system must rely upon external sources for change.[10] In any case, it is clear that the guidelines of the curriculum bulletins developed by the bureau staff and the deputy superintendent are extremely influential.

Assistant superintendents who head the school divisions at headquarters (i.e., high school, junior high school, and elementary school) sometimes participate in the development of curriculum policy through devising experimental curriculum programs. Such programs are developed on an *ad hoc* basis, but may result in a permanent change if there is effective follow-through in evaluating them. Generally, however, experimentation is limited, and evaluation has been ineffective. Under the present structure, each of these functions is performed by a separate headquarters staff, and communication between the agencies is severely limited. Evaluation of curriculum is almost never made except as such evaluation is part of larger programs, i.e., Higher Horizons or the More Effective Schools program. This separation of the research, evaluation, and curriculum development functions cuts off the possible sources of innovation from the curriculum policymakers. It is indicative of the narrow spheres of operation and reference of the headquarters staff.[11]

Finally, what about the public? Interest groups rarely participate in curriculum decisions. The school system's defense of the need for professional expertise is probably most extreme in the area of curriculum development. Further, most potential participants among the public simply assume that the school system knows its business. There are, therefore, limited pressures for alternative policies and innovation. On several occasions, however, groups have lobbied for inclusion of particular items in the curriculum. For example, civil rights groups recently succeeded in securing the inclusion of Negro history in the social studies curriculum. The United Parents Association and Public Education Association supported their efforts. Two new bulletins in this general area were issued to teachers in 1965, "The Negro in American History" and "Puerto Rican Profiles." The Catholic Teachers Association periodically registers complaints about approved textbooks or bibliographies.

For all practical purposes, however, the continuing participants in curriculum policymaking are the professionals at headquarters. The deputy superintendent and the assistant superintendent in charge of the Bureau of Curriculum Research are the key initiators of policy, and the curriculum coordinators its implementors — even though principals and teachers are the final determinants of what is done in the schools and the classrooms.

CHAPTER V

The Arena Widens:
Bargaining in Selecting a Superintendent
and Setting a Salary Policy

In two areas of policy, salary increases and selection of the superintendent, there is limited participation by individuals outside the school system. In the selection of the superintendent, the Board of Education plays a primary role; salary policy has involved the United Federation of Teachers, the mayor, and to some extent local labor leaders.

Selection of the Superintendent

The process of appointing a superintendent is a key area of policymaking too often overlooked in analyses of power.[1] A chief executive can potentially do much to shape the character of the bureaucracy he administers. The degree to which he assumes power and the techniques he uses to implement policy often will depend upon who selects him and what his relationship is with others who hold power within the same system. Whether or not he will initiate or support change in the system, and his receptiveness to public pressures and alternative policies, are also conditioned by the method of appointment. The general calibre of the appointee is very much a product of the selection process.

In the institutional setting of the school system, the most significant appointments are the Board members and the superintendent. As already noted, administrative appointments under the superintendent are circumscribed by examination and tenure procedures. For the purpose of the present study, which sought to define the influences within a political subsystem, the selection of the superintendent was the most appropriate appointment process to examine.

A review of appointments in the first part of the century indicates that the mayor was actively involved in the selection of the superintendent and in several instances actually made the appointment. However, the president of the Board has been the single most persistent and influential participant in the selection process. In earlier years, this was undoubtedly due to the mayor's strong support of the president, who was his appointee. Though no longer appointed by the mayor, the president has continued to maintain an authoritative position of influence.

Repeatedly, the most important issue raised in the choice of a superintendent has been whether he should be from within or without the system. This concern is obviously a constant issue in bureaucratic appointments in general, and the behavior of the administrative bureaucracy in the New York City school system follows the expected pattern: it has always strongly supported the appointment of someone from within its own ranks. The Board of Education has responded to that interest favorably. In the case of the four most recent appointments (there have been nine superintendents altogether), two superintendents were chosen from within the system, a third was a local college president,[2] and one was an outsider.

The religious background of the superintendent has not been a major issue. The only instance of a religious issue being raised was in relation to a candidate who was considered unacceptable to the Catholic Church because he had opposed free bussing for parochial school children. Of the nine superintendents to date, two were Catholic; no Jew has ever served as superintendent.

The four most recent appointments were given systematic analyses. Each involved a narrow group of participants. In each instance, the Public Education Association made a concerted effort to influence the choice. The Association repeatedly encouraged the Board to establish an independent selection panel comprised of professionals who would search the country for potential candidates and make recommendations to the Board. (The Public Education Association not only felt greater confidence in the recommendations of a professional panel but saw itself as being more influential in such a process, since the Association's strong professional ties would provide it with a direct line to the panel.)

In March 1946, the Board responded affirmatively to the Association's pressures and named a screening committee headed by Dr. William H. Kirkpatrick (Professor Emeritus of Education at Teachers College). In October, the committee presented a list of six candidates to the Board. Three were outsiders whom the committee rated, and three were unrated insiders. The supervisory staff at headquarters responded by urging the appointment of a local person, preferably from within its own ranks.[3] The Public Education Association suggested that the Kirkpatrick Committee rank all the candidates in order of preference, so that they could be considered on the basis of personal qualification rather than on whether they were insiders or outsiders. Suspicious that the Board would consider only local candidates, the Association also requested that the Board make a public statement explaining the basis for its selection. A limited public discussion of the issues took place, centering on the question of insider versus outsider.

Ultimately, the appointee was an insider who had come up through the ranks and had served as the top assistant to the retiring superintendent. The designated superintendent had been ranked last by the panel. The appointment represented the personal preference of the Board president. The vote was reported by the newspaper as four to three with the latter three votes being cast for the outsider who had received the highest recommendation of the panel. A prominent member of the Board (who had cast one of the three losing votes) protested the action, declaring that provincialism and politics had served to exclude an outsider as a choice for superintendent. He is quoted as saying: "We did not appraise the men listed with reference to particular fitness for the post."[4]

The Public Education Association was ready to do battle with the Board again on the next appointment, approximately ten years later. On the announcement of the imminent retirement of the incumbent superintendent, the Association formed a coordinating committee. Speaking for eighteen generally influential city-wide civic organizations, it requested that the Board announce the procedure to be used in selecting the next superintendent. It recommended, at the same time, the appointment of an advisory commitee to assist in recruiting and screening candidates. The president of the Board agreed to take the matter under advisement. Privately, Board members indicated to each other that they had little faith that a nationwide search would produce a better candidate than could be found in the city's school system.

During a ten-month period, from December 1956 to September 1957, the Association's coordinating committee continued to pressure the Board president in a series of letters requesting the appointment of a selection panel. The president eschewed discussion of the request. Meanwhile, the supervisory staff again indicated its support for a local candidate. In September, the Board invited interested groups to suggest possible candidates. Seven days after that announcement, *The New York Times* reported that the deputy mayor of the city (who had formerly been president of a city college) had applied to the state Department of Education for a superintendent's certificate. In December, he was appointed superintendent of schools. The Board president and the mayor were close political associates, and the selection of the superintendent was obviously a decision reached in consultation with the mayor.

The superintendent's candidacy was strongly supported by the Board president, and there was no opposition from within the Board itself.[5]

The selection of the next superintendent, in 1962, was distinguished by the fact that members of a new Board of Education had been nominated by a civic screening panel. A special advisory committee chosen by the Board and headed by Francis Keppel (then Dean of the School of Education at Harvard), unanimously recommended a candidate from outside New York City. The supervisory staff indicated its usual support for a local person. The Board accepted the judgment of its panel. Its appointment of a superintendent from outside the system was a fulfillment of the aims of the Public Education Association, which had been bypassed by all previous Boards.

The superintendent, however, was dismissed less than two years after taking office. This dismissal undoubtedly had a strong effect upon the choice of the next superintendent. The Public Education Association abandoned its commitment to an appointment from outside the city. The administrative bureaucracy was not reluctant to indicate that its desire for an appointee from within the system had now been justified. In 1964 the Board returned to its earlier approach and selected the highest ranking insider as superintendent. There was no opposition. The candidate had served as acting superintendent, he had come up through the ranks, and he was next in line for the job.

The selection of the superintendent is likely to be the most important policy decision made by the Board of Education, and the president of the Board is, therefore, a primary participant in the process. There can be little doubt that no superintendent would be chosen of whom he did not approve. At the same time, the strongest institutional influence on the Board is the bureaucracy's pressure for an appointment of someone reared in the system. That pressure is direct and overt. It takes the form of direct recommendations in the public pronouncements of the various supervisory associations. Not unimportant, too, are the suggestions of individual members of the bureaucracy that are solicited by Board members. The appointment of the superintendent so vitally affects the bureaucracy's vested interests that its concern is understandable. Given the city's recent experience, with its one outsider, the bureaucracy's pressure for the appointment of a top ranking insider will be even more influential in the immediate future.

It is clear that such a selection process is exceedingly important in shaping the scope of educational policy as a whole. At the very least, the current procedure does not encourage an opening of channels but rather reinforces the narrow participation characteristic of functional specialization.

Teachers' Salaries

The determination of teachers' salaries was chosen for examination because of the growing importance of teachers organizations, not only in New York but as a rule in all large cities. Thus, there is a need to reevaluate the role of such organizations in setting educational policy. Although it appeared self-evident that in general there would be no broad public participation in salary negotiations, it nonetheless seemed worthwhile to study the strategy and tactics of the few participants involved.

In New York City, the establishing of salary scales and related benefits for teachers has undergone a major adjustment in the last six years. Prior to the election of the United Federation of Teachers in 1959 as the recognized collective-bargaining agent for the city's 51,000 school teachers, the Board of Education had the upper hand in determining salary policy. The multiplicity of relatively weak groups representing teachers diffused the pressure on the Board and the mayor.[6] But in the last three salary negotiations (1961, 1963, and 1965), the Union has demonstrated its growing importance in policy-making.

The Union's accomplishments as a policy participant are reflected in substantial salary increases and in its success in achieving its stated goals. Negotiated contracts, largely a product of Union ingenuity, have become major policy documents for the city's school system. These documents have implications far beyond salary questions. In fact, the Board has always pressed for a ruling that will limit negotiations only to questions of salary. The Union has been successful in including other matters it considers to be directly related to salary policy.

The contract negotiated between the Board of Education and the United Federation of Teachers in 1965 marked the largest settlement ever won by the city's teachers — and very probably by any teacher organization in the country. It provided for an average salary increase of $800 over two years, raising the average salary to $9,300. (The previous contract had given teachers an average salary increase of $580.) Other features of the settlement provided for increases in maximum salary from $11,025 to $11,950, reduction in maximum class size from 35 to 33 in elementary and junior high schools and from 39 to 36 in high schools, and increases in the number of preparation periods for teachers in elementary schools. (See Tables XIV and XV, Appendix A.)

The conflict between the Board and the Union in 1965 was evident in the wide gap between demands and offers. The package offered by the mayor's mediation panel was closer to the Union's position. Indeed, in its earliest negotiations with the superintendent and the Board president, the Union's settlement offer was actually less than the final settlement proposed by the panel.

The time schedule established by the Board to allow for salary and contract negotiations is particularly relevant to understanding the pressures in this area. A contract which must be negotiated by September when school opens may not be discussed until the summer of that year. Serious negotiations may be delayed until after the city budget is final and that may not occur until late June. As with most education budgets, the Board's estimate usually contains no provision for salary increases. A Union official has suggested that the Board does not like to negotiate early in the year because it assumes that the Union would then have greater flexibility in raising its demands before the budget is final. It is more likely that the Board feels that by delaying settlement, it can shift the responsibility for meeting negotiated salary costs to the city. Whatever the motivation, the procedure tends to undermine the superintendent's role in negotations while it encourages the participation of the mayor.

Strikes and the threat of strikes have been effectively utilized by the United Federation of Teachers to secure salary increases and an acceptable contract. Strikes were threatened in May 1960, in 1963, and in 1965. Strike action was taken in November 1960 and April 1962. Early strikes served the purpose of solidifying the U.F.T.'s position and increasing its membership lists. In the future, though, it is unlikely that Union leaders will be inclined to resort to strike action quite so readily. As an established and accepted institution, the Union probably will tend to seek regularized bargaining procedures. Indicative of the Union's recognition of its changing role is its recent pressure on the Board to adopt arbitration.

In reviewing the procedures in the setting of salary policy since 1959, it is apparent that decisions were made by a core of schoolmen together with the active involvement of political and labor leaders. Each year the superintendent and Board president generally agree that no increases can be anticipated that year. (Only once did the superintendent — who then was newly-appointed and from outside the system — initially admit to the possibility of conducting negotiations, and his offer was later undermined by the Board.) Meetings with the Union's officers, the superintendent, the Board president, and some representatives of the mayor generally follow. In all three negotiations, a major labor leader in the city was instrumental in bringing the parties together and, in fact, sat in on the discussions. The first mediation panel appointed by the mayor, in 1961, was comprised of three of the city's top union leaders. (In that year the mayor was involved in a primary-election fight, and his support of the Union proposal was published in its newspaper several days before the election.) In 1962 the governor and the state commissioner of education were drawn into the negotiations by the Union because of the need to work out a financial arrangement under the state-aid formula.

In 1963 the mayor again appointed a three-member mediation panel because of the failure of the Board and the Union to reach any agreement. (The selection of the members showed that the mayor was responsive to the recommendations of the Union president.) The panel again prepared the settlement package. In 1965 summer negotiation meetings were held with the acting Board president, the superintendent, an assistant to the mayor, and Union leaders. The mayor himself later called the group in for discussions. The superintendent set up a meeting with Union officials, indicating a settlement could be reached; a subsequent meeting in his office led to an agreement that was later abandoned. The mayor's mediators were called on to secure a settlement.

In these three instances, then, the mayor's "mediators" acted not as mediators but rather as an arbitration group preparing the actual terms for settlement. On all three occasions, the Union's stated policy program provided the basis for the panel's deliberations.

Board members have claimed that the mayor becomes involved in these negotiations on his own initiative and that they would prefer to settle the contract on their own. Most of the evidence, however, suggests that the Board shifts final salary negotiations to the mayor, albeit as a result of its inability to reach a settlement. Union leaders admit to their bargaining advantage in dealing with the mayor, although their preference now appears to be for more regularized procedures.

The supervisory bureaucracy does not participate directly in salary negotiations except to the extent that the budget officer estimates costs for salary adjustments. These estimates are never intended to be realistic and are not, therefore, particularly significant. There is indirect administrative support for teachers' salary increases because of their potential effect on administrative salaries. The Council of Supervisory Associations was organized in 1962 to keep track of teachers' salary negotiations and assure comparable increases in administrative salaries. An index established in 1962 by state law (over the objections of the mayor and the Board) guarantees automatic proportionate increases for supervisors.[7]

In at least two instances the superintendent was directly involved in salary negotiations. In 1962 the superintendent, fighting for his job, set out to accomplish a settlement with the Union by enlisting financial support from the mayor to cover the increases. In 1965 the incumbent superintendent (who served as a negotiator for the High School Teachers Association in the late 1950's) was an active participant, keeping in constant touch with the Board president and the mayor's representative. In both instances, however, final settlements were not made until the mayor became involved.

The period covered in this analysis of salary policy may be distorted some- what by the special circumstances of the recent recognition of the Union and the relatively low level of teachers' salaries in 1960. There is the possibility that the Board's role as negotiator was undermined during the initial period of the Union's emergence and that some of the control it formerly exercised will be gradually restored. However, the Union has been singularly successful in setting salary policy, and it is unlikely that its role will be radically changed. In fact, it is rather more likely that established salary arbitration procedures will encourage Union involvement in other areas of school policy. In any case, so far as salary is concerned, since the large increases achieved during the last six years have raised the city's teachers to a more competitive level, it is prob- able that further increases will be gradual and achieved through closer cooper- ation.

CHAPTER VI

Professionals Under Public Pressure: Integration Policy and Obstacles to Implementation

School integration policy has become one of the most important and sensitive areas of school decision making. The Supreme Court decision in 1954 exposed school systems to public review and attracted wide participation in the discussion of school integration. The highly-charged emotional impact of the issue was one of the reasons for the active response. The major pressure in New York City for the Board to take a position on this issue was external, a direct outgrowth of the court decision. Conflict on the Board and indecision in the administrative bureaucracy obstructed clarification of the Board's policy. However, the lack of firm city and Board leadership and commitment encouraged further public and interest-group participation.

Board policy, when first adopted in 1957, had strong interest-group support. It set as its goals quality education and integrated schools, and was based on 26 recommendations of a Board commission comprised of 15 members representing the city administration, the school bureaucracy, and special-interest groups.[1] A proposal for teacher rotation raised some controversy as did a recommendation for rezoning to achieve integrated schools. The major civic groups, however, responded positively to all of the recommendations, lending full support to their adoption.[2] Although several Board members were not committed to the two controversial proposals of teacher rotation and rezoning, the Board finally adopted all of them. The recommendations were stated in broad policy terms, and administrative implementation was delegated to the superintendent and his staff. Basically, implementation rested on three mechanisms: zoning, site selection and school construction, and pupil redistribution.

It is possible that if implementation had been immediate and firm, the strong civic-group support for the early recommendations would have been sufficient to carry forth the plan, and opposition might have been minimized. But delay and postponement allowed time for opposition coalitions to develop. Initially, civil rights groups responded favorably to the Board's policy, averring that they considered it to be the most comprehensive proposal adopted in any city. Within the year, however, the Urban League and the N.A.A.C.P. became severely critical of the inaction of the superintendent and the headquarters staff. The Board's commission and other civic groups also decried the delay in implementation.[3]

As noted, teacher rotation and rezoning were the most controversial elements in the Board's policy. Within a year of the Board's adoption of its integration policy, a Negro clergyman and civil rights leader, the Reverend Milton Galamison, proceeded to test the superintendent's intentions by requesting a rezoning of a segregated junior high school in Brooklyn. Galamison, pastor of the Siloam Presbyterian Church in the lower-class Negro neighborhood of Bedford-Stuyvesant in Brooklyn (the church is the largest in the Brooklyn-Nassau Presbytery), was later to become the most militant school integrationist in the city and the leader of a school boycott in 1964. In response to Galamison's request, the superintendent issued a public statement suggesting that the neighborhood school concept would not be sacrificed to integration goals. This forced both the Urban League and the N.A.A.C.P. to condemn the superintendent publicly. The statement increased the determination of civil rights groups to stress school integration as their goal. The Board president continued to espouse strong commitment to school integration. The superintendent and the staff, however, made no effort to develop plans toward that end. Indicative of staff inaction was the final report of the retiring superintendent in 1958 (William Jansen), that made no mention of progress or plans for school integration. The teachers groups, in the meantime, convinced the superintendent that a voluntary teacher rotation program was all that was necessary to encourage experienced teachers to serve in ghetto schools. In the first year, 25 teachers volunteered for these assignments.

The new superintendent (John Theobald), appointed in June 1958, set out on a piecemeal program of trial integration. Soon after his appointment, he announced a rezoning plan for several Brooklyn and Queens school districts that was to involve the transfer of 2,000 children. The controversy which developed was to recur on each occasion of announced plans for some form of school integration.

Sixteen schools were involved in the proposed rezoning, six in the lower-class Negro neighborhood of Bedford-Stuyvesant, six in other white lower-class Brooklyn neighborhoods, three in white lower-class Ridgewood (Queens) and one in the lower-middle-class neighborhood of Glendale (Queens). The maximum distance to be traveled was 3.1 miles; children living over one mile away were to be provided with free bus transportation. Thirty-four civic groups supported the superintendent's decision, as did *The New York Times*. A local citizens group voiced its opposition and presented an alternative plan that was rejected by a Board committee. On June 24, 1959, the superintendent stated that his original plan still stood. During that same week, local parents groups protested at city hall and several elected officials entered the controversy.

A state senator from Queens complained that the Board had not prepared the community sufficiently for the change. The Queens borough president and a local councilman met with the mayor to register their concern. The City Commission on Integroup Relations announced that it had been working with the Brooklyn and Queens groups and was confident the transfer could be accomplished in an orderly manner.

By the end of July, however, within a month after this announcement was made, the number of students to be transferred was reduced from 2,000 to 400, and still formal protests to the Board multiplied. Local opposition groups were organized, and their protests became louder. The American Jewish Congress and United Parents Association called on the Board to act immediately to achieve the rezoning. But on July 27, the vice president of the Board questioned whether the superintendent could take such action without Board approval. Other members of the Board supported his position. On August 15, the Board reluctantly backed the superintendent's plan, but the split on the Board was evident. The president, for the first time since the initial adoption of an integration policy, announced the Board's commitment to the neighborhood school concept. He stated that the superintendent's plan was temporary — that the 400 children eventually would be transferred back — and the purpose of the Board's policy was not integration but equal educational opportunity. Dissatisfied with the Board's action, five mothers appealed the decision to the state education commissioner. The commissioner refused to prevent the Board from transferring the students. On September 5, in response to a parents group opposing the transfer, the Brooklyn Supreme Court asked the Board to show cause why the pupil transfer plan should not be stayed. Parent strikes against the Board were held for two days in the local community. At approximately the same time, the Board announced the construction of a new school in the Negro area of Bedford-Stuyvesant, and the transfer plan was abandoned.[4]

Thus, in this two-month period, delay and indecision in the inner circle of educational decision makers fostered confused concern and resentment in the community. Original Board and staff policy was compromised in response to the protests of a small group of parents. The neighborhood school became the first line of defense of those who opposed rezoning and transfer. The headquarters staff fully supported the concept of the neighborhood school, and staff inaction was in effect a veto of Board policy. Public statements by the various supervisory associations opposing any new plans for rezoning or school transfers were indicative of the staff's position. Subsequently, the Council of Supervisory Associations opposed the abandonment of the I.Q. tests, the school pairing plan, and school reorganization. The elementary, junior high, and high school principals' associations all stated their opposition to any program that required children to be moved out of neighborhood schools against their parents' will.[5]

Over the next several years, the integrationists turned to active support of rezoning and transfer of students, emphasizing school integration as a means of achieving equal educational opportunity. Parents groups in Harlem and Bedford-Stuyvesant set out on a series of requests for school transfers, and kept their children out of school while seeking a legal justification for their position. Generally the courts held that parents who kept their children out of school were guilty of neglect. In several instances, however, the court noted the inferior quality of education in the ghetto schools.[6]

In 1960 the split on the Board became one reason it failed to respond to public pressures that it adopt a timetable for implementing its policy goals, now three years old. Open-enrollment plans were offered as the new implementation panacea.[7] This program called for the voluntary transfer of nonwhite children to white schools. Civic and civil rights groups cheered the announcement of a list of sending and receiving schools. The superintendent made clear, however, that he was still partial to the neighborhood school. In all, fewer than 10 per cent of those eligible to transfer under open enrollment took advantage of the program. Of a total eligible group of 20,000 students, 677 transferred.[8] It was apparent, however, that civic-group support and administrative policy were now committed to voluntary transfer of Negroes to white schools.[9]

Although the new Board of Education, appointed in 1961, included in its membership several supporters of stronger integration policy, no radical changes in implementation were forthcoming.[10] In July of 1961, the superintendent issued the first progress report on implementation of the school system's 1957 school integration policy. The report was more a statement of the complexity of the problem than a description of meaningful accomplishment.[11]

In the next year, the original coalition of support for integration gradually disintegrated and was further undermined by the lack of resolve on the part of the new Board and the headquarters staff to force the implementation of policy. The mayor repeatedly refused to become involved. The opposition coalition, on the other hand, was encouraged by state legislators and city councilmen. Further, the piecemeal efforts of the educational administration had enabled the local opposition groups to muster support and project their demands. A forthcoming study of the desegregation issue in New York City describes the opposition coalition as composed of white parents, real estate interests, and school officials, all of whom rallied around the neighborhood school concept. The supporters of Board policy, the study suggests, were unable to organize grass roots support, and lacked the unity necessary to encourage implementation. This study sees the failure of moderate groups in the city to support integration as being particularly significant.[12] My own more limited research accords with these conclusions.

In 1962 the superintendent's office proposed that 24 schools be paired. Following the pattern of previous piecemeal efforts, by the time the plan was made final, the number of schools was reduced to four. Leaders at United Parents Association proudly took credit for the reduction. Actually they had worked with headquarters staff to rationalize the conclusion that the pairing of most of the schools would not be advantageous. The headquarters staff was obviously receptive to this reduction, if not instrumental in securing it.

The complete frustration in implementing the Board's original plans was indicated in the conclusions of the 1964 Allen Commission Report, that evaluated the progress of school integration in New York City. It noted that between 1959 and 1963, only 100 changes in districts and zones were made. Open enrollment, the report stated, had no significant effect, and plans for school construction were clearly reinforcing the pattern of segregation.[13] Further, as the staff floundered with makeshift arrangements, ethnic changes in the city's schools increased the magnitude of the problem, and the number of predominantly Negro and Puerto Rican schools increased.[14] In general, the report concluded, in the eight years since 1957, implementation policy in all three initial areas of focus — zoning, site selection and school construction, and pupil redistribution — was negligible.

The first long-range staff program designed to achieve implementation of Board policy was published in a report by the superintendent in March 1965.[15] It followed very soon after the report of the state education commissioner. The Board's emphasis was now shifted to school reorganization. The intermediate school, the comprehensive high school, and the educational parks were the new panacea. This new emphasis was a concession to the retention of the neighborhood school concept, shifting the burden of student redistribution to the junior and senior high schools. The time schedule for institution of the reorganization was set for 1972-73. Since the publication of the report, the superintendent has announced that the program is actually experimental and will proceed at a slow pace.

The school integration issue is the only area in which public response has been vociferous and active. It has attracted the widest public participation of any of the five policy decisions explored here, and probably the widest public participation of any educational issue of the past two decades. Local groups of every shade of opinion have organized to oppose or defend individual plans. Among the most vociferous have been PAT, (the Parents and Taxpayers Association) and their opposite number, EQUAL, (Parents and Neighbors United for Integrated-Quality Education). Civil rights groups entered the school policy field with the single concern of achieving an integrated system. They have since concentrated their efforts on improving the quality of the schools. Local civic groups, chambers of commerce, councilmen, and candidates for public office have voiced strong opinions on proposals. Many of these groups and individuals have never before been involved in school affairs, and their current concern has been limited to the integration issue and its ramifications.

All this interest has produced perhaps the most significant development in school decision making. For the past two decades, superintendents, boards, and school bureaucracies have been freewheeling, with little outside pressure, more or less entirely independent of public opinion. They have successfully closed off school policy formulation from elected local government officials and civic groups. The integration issue now has broken open the monopoly of power vested in this small core of school officials. It has raised serious questions regarding the role of professionals, their goals and interests in school policy.

CHAPTER VII

Public Government and Public Education

This description of selected areas of decision making reflects how much of what happens in the school system is a matter of routine procedure. It suggests the limited alternatives offered and/or considered by those who make formal policy, particularly the core of school professionals.

One could accurately describe the situation in New York City over the past two decades as an abandonment of public education by key forces of potential power within the city. Max Weber's theory of the emergence of a specialized bureaucracy monopolizing power through its control of expertise describes the role of the education bureaucracy in New York City. The claim that only the professionals can make competent judgments has been accepted by the public. Contributing to and perhaps an outgrowth of this acceptance is the change in the mayor's role in educational matters from one of active participation to one of restricted involvement. Civic and interest groups (other than the specialized education groups) have responded to the situation ambivalently; on the one hand they accept the notion of the professional competence of the bureaucracy but, on the other hand, they express a hopelessness regarding their ability to change the system. The end result is narrow or closed participation in large areas of nonvisible decision making, in which effective influence is restricted to an inside core of top supervisory personnel in the headquarters staff of the Board of Education.

Innovation and responsiveness to change are difficult to build into any bureaucratic system, and education policy in New York City partly reflects that circumstance. But at the same time, there are forces *external* to the system that can serve as catalysts for change.[1] The following is a description of two such forces, the state and city governments.[2]

The State

State minimum standards for education are not an overriding influence on a large city such as New York, which tends to make even greater demands on itself than does the state. What influence the state exerts results from the state-aid formula, the Regents' policy, and the administrative rulings of the state education commissioner. In regard to the latter, recent studies in other states have emphasized the increasing importance of the state bureaucracy in local educational policy, particularly the role of the commissioner.[3]

In recent years, the state commissioner has been involved in two major policy decisions affecting New York City. He was instrumental in the removal of the entire Board of Education in 1961. Subsequently he recommended the change in procedure for selecting the new Board. In 1958, his condemnation of *de facto* segregation in New York City was a catalyst to the reevaluation of how Board policy on school integration was being implemented. He continued to influence city policy in this regard by outlining the problems of school segregation in a series of reports.[4] In addition to these more overt actions, the commissioner's influence is felt in his informal contacts with the superintendent and the staff.[5]

For its part, the city itself has been notably ineffectual as a force in Albany. One study attributes this failure to the splintering of city educational interest groups. The New York State Educational Conference Board is the strongest and most influential coalition of interest groups in the determination of state education policy, and city interests are meagerly represented on the board. Thus, in effect, the state has been able to ignore city education needs without serious political consequences.[6] The general deficiency in leadership in public education in New York is reflected in part in its failure to significantly influence state policy.

The City

The most significant trend in education in New York City over the past two decades has been the isolation of school administration from the city government. In almost every city administration since the 1940's, complaints of undue city interference — usually described as "political" interference — have resulted in the delegation of increased responsibility to the Board of Education. The National Education Association condemned Mayor LaGuardia for direct interference with the school system, particularly in personnel policy; the institution of a strict merit system and internal controls over promotions and transfers prevented future mayors from engaging in similar practices. In 1951, the Strayer-Yavner Report, a major report on the city's educational system, concluded that education policy was controlled by the Board of Estimate, the mayor, and (because of the line-item budget) the budget director of the city.[7] Subsequently the lump-sum budget was adopted, giving the professionals complete control over allocation of funds.[8] Complaints about a "political"

Board toward the end of the 50's were satisfied by the institution of the civic selection panel.[9]

But it is the increased bureaucratization and overblown professionalization of the school system that has had the greatest impact on school policymaking. The professional bureaucracy has manipulated its resources of expertise to discourage opposition and competing policies. The public's acceptance of technical expertise as the most relevant, if not the only, basis for sound judgment has furthered the depoliticalization of education policy.

The depoliticalization process has been a two-way street. Detailed review of newspaper items over the last five years substantiate the intention of the last previous mayor (Robert Wagner) to remove himself from educational policymaking.[10] His public statements were always worded in general terms, supporting more and better schools. He specifically avoided policy positions on controversial school issues. On school integration, he repeatedly stated his desire to leave the matter to the Board of Education and the professional staff. "I subscribe without reservation to the goals of quality integrated education in our schools and of equal opportunity for every child," he once is quoted as saying. "But the plan, the means, the how, where and what — the timetable, the specific approaches and programs — that is for the educators and for the Board to determine."[11] During the most heated periods of controversy, he met with protest groups but repeatedly refused to intervene.

Requests to the Mayor from the Board of Education in 1964 for $45.3 million in additional funds for a "More Effective Schools" program drew him to the fringe of the integration issue. The proposal called for obtaining additional funds and for services for ten schools in ghetto areas. Ultimately, his decision favoring a smaller appropriation was reached after consultation with school officials and staff members of educational interest groups. The Mayor was drawn into such an issue only on the rare occasions that additional financial support was sought, or when the Board and some other city agency came into a conflict that had to be reviewed and resolved before the Board of Estimate. (An aide to Mayor Wagner maintained that the Mayor himself viewed his actions as shifting responsibility for the determination of education policy to the Board of Education: "The Mayor did not want to get involved with school problems.")

The Mayor's general policy of noninvolvement was reinforced by two major changes in procedure instituted during his administration: the lump-sum appropriation of school funds and the panel selection of Board members.

Under a local law first passed in 1962 and reenacted each year since then, and by way of a memorandum of understanding with the mayor, the Board has the power to determine its own allocation of funds. Post-audit control is also an internal operation, controlled largely by the top supervisory staff. Thus, mayoral influence is kept to an absolute minimum. The Board of Education is the only agency in New York City with such budgetary independence from the municipal government.

As for the selection of Board members, it has already been noted that prior to 1961 Board appointments were made directly by the mayor. Under the new procedure, the nine members of the Board are appointed by the mayor from a screened list of candidates submitted by a selection panel composed of the heads of eleven educational, civic, and professional organizations. This change in procedure was established in an effort to deter "political" appointments. It followed six years of hearings, numerous scandals, and finally the removal of the Board by the state legislature.

Currently, the mayor's office takes part in school policy in two general situations. The first concerns issues on which conflict between major participants cannot be compromised without the mayor's involvement. Such issues often concern site selection and provoke sharp differences between the City Planning Commission and the Board. The second is when key participants decide they will gain by the mayor's direct participation, such as has been the case in salary negotiations.

One of the obvious questions which arises in connection with the Mayor's role in education policy is whether the precedents established over a 12-year period, under the Wagner Administration, are somehow integral to the structure of big-city government. Significantly, Mayor Wagner's role conforms to Banfield's portrait of the mayor of Chicago as a mediator of conflicts rather than an initiator of policy,[12] suggesting that a general process is at work here. On the other hand, a mayor elected on a reform platform who therefore cannot rely on party backing may be less likely to accept the role of mediator and, in fact, often uses his power to initiate policy to encourage new political support.

Perhaps the most important element in such considerations is the fact that mayoral noninvolvement is in part a result of both elite and public deference to professionalism. Such an attitude is by no means limited to the educational bureaucracy. The current mayor of New York, Mayor Lindsay, in his short tenure in office, has already faced the charge of "political interference" in an attempt to initiate policy in the creation of a civilian police review board. The Mayor's involvement in a local school crisis brought forth a statement from the Board that they were a state agency and would not tolerate his interference with school matters. The emotional commitment to professionalism, although not inviolate, tends to oppose any attempts to promote new policies or alternate courses of action as "political interference." Of course, in the case of Lindsay, a new mayor, his efforts to reassert a policy role with regard to the schools represent a direct threat to those who have held almost complete power in school decision making.

Public Participation

Public participation in policymaking can come through two obvious channels, voting and/or organized interest groups. In New York City there are no public votes on school issues. The assumption that voting *in itself* automatically assures meaingful public participation has long been abandoned. Within the context of a specialized area of decision making, such as education, the extent of public participation must be measured in terms of the influence exerted by various public interest groups and elected officials. These two bodies are the only possible source of policy alternatives.

Elected officials in New York City play a relatively insignificant role in education policymaking. Public interest is equally low. Indicatively, while two newspapers in the city report regularly on education matters, criticism of the system in both has been mild and infrequent. Ethnic and religious groups for their part have been satisfied with adequate representation on the Board and in the bureaucracy. (Catholic groups intermittently become concerned with textbooks and curriculum but rely on the Catholic Teachers Association and on personal contact with the Board to make their basically minor demands.[13])

As for the wealthy, they or their representatives have supported ever-increasing expenditures in education, but have removed themselves from all other considerations of policy. There are no economic "notables" in New York City identified with public education; no one who can be considered under this rubric has served on the Board of Education. Similarly, the "civic do-gooders" concerned with educational matters have worked to alleviate problems which are a product of inadequate educational policy rather than to assure the development of sound practices.[14]

Public participation in school policy formulation is circumscribed by the lack of visible decision making, the general shortage of information available to the public, and a deficiency in the means for participation. While parent associations are active in individual schools with regard to localized and personalized problems, the highly centralized organization of the school system is a serious deterrent to communication between parent groups and policy-makers. In short, public education policy has become the province of the professional bureaucrat, with the tragic result that the *status quo,* suffering from many difficulties, is the order of the day.

CHAPTER VIII

Diagnosis and Prescription

Functional Specialization and School Policy

In a rather concise — and, one might say, almost modest — characterization of the educational world in New York City, Sayre and Kaufman noted: "On balance, the school official enjoys an unusual capacity for self-government."[1]

In fact, with the exception of the integration issue, there are only three or four areas in which *any* appreciable outside influence is brought to bear on matters of education policy. Such influence is most direct in regard to the religious and racial balance on the Board of Education and in the distribution of appointments to the supervisory staff. To these items should be added the mayor's role in the determination of teachers' salaries. Some outside influence can also be seen in the negotiations for individual school locations, the bargaining for school construction contracts, and the granting of minor favors by local district superintendents (in their limited sphere of operation). Basically, however, there are no forces acting to broaden education policy and balance it with other city policy.

As a political subsystem, the New York City school system can only be described as "narrow, convergent and dominated by a consensual elite."[2] This description is in sharp contrast to the usual view of New York City politics as "open" — or to the somewhat typical suggestion in this instance by Sayre and Kaufman that "no part of the city's large and varied population is alienated from participation in the system."[3]

For the political scientist, such a disparity poses a basic problem in creating meaningful operational categories by which power can be analyzed. The results of this study indicate the real need to examine how power is exercised in individual areas of activity. Such examinations should explore differences in the distribution of power, in the kinds and levels of participation, the degree of integration by city-wide elements, and the role of nonprofessional and nonsupportive interest groups. Working from this type of analysis, the methodological concern with pluralist and power elite concepts may be shifted to the development of more quantitative measurements of the determinants of open and closed political systems. Such an approach will also provide greater insights into the sources and possibilities for change in a political system.[4]

This approach is not unlike the position presented by Norton Long in "The Local Community as an Ecology of Games," which stresses defining the territorial limits of local political operations (or games).[5] The territorial limits here are defined as areas of functional specialization. David Minar has also moved in the general direction of such an approach, suggesting that in the study of school districts, classifications should relate to technical versus rank authority domination, thereby distinguishing between nonparticipation and participation by other than school professionals.[6] In a unifunctional type of analysis, Minar notes, concern should be focused on "whether opposed, not complementary groups outside the authority system attempt to exert influence on the decision making process."[7] Information of this sort can be derived only through a functional analyses of power.

Implications for Other School Systems

Norton Long in reviewing the Sayre-Kaufman study of New York City justifiably criticised the authors for their emphasis on the uniqueness of New York City.[8] A case study should aim at providing leads for more generalized observations. With such an objective in view, it is important to note that some of the findings in the present study challenge basic concepts in educational thinking about large city school systems. For example, New York City, though designated as a fiscally "dependent" district, is quite *independent* in its control over educational policy, including its financing. The results of this study, then, should indicate to professional educators the barrenness of the usual understanding of fiscally independent and dependent districts.[9]

This study further suggests that current developments in larger cities indicate a need for more not less "outside" public influence in school systems. Although there is a dearth of data on policymaking in large city school systems (or on school systems in general), certain hypotheses, worthy of verification, can be advanced. It appears that the size of a city is an important determinant in the degree to which internal bureaucratic control is sought and the influence of the public and public officials is avoided. From the school studies which now exist, it seems clear that there is greater involvement on the part of political notables in smaller communities. In larger cities, both political and economic notables tend to be more occupied with state and federal policy.[9a] (Also many of them may be active in suburban school politics, or their children may be in private schools.) Thus, if an index of bureaucratization could be developed, it would probably indicate a higher ratio of bureaucratization in certain of the larger cities.

It is almost certain that in larger cities curriculum, budgeting, and personnel policy are controlled completely by a headquarters bureaucracy. In addition, the isolation of the school systems from the rest of city government has undoubtedly occured, in cities large and small. As Minar suggests: "the organizational and ideological independence of the school system is both symbolic and supportive of this isolation."[10]

Lack of responsiveness to change and defense of the *status quo* are natural outgrowths of the "closed" policymaking that exists within school systems.[11] The character of school decision making as reflected in the area of desegregation provides specific evidence of the restraints that prevent and weaken adjustments to vast changes in the school clientele. (In most of the large cities, the school bureaucracy itself, particularly the headquarters staff, has been a primary force in preventing implementation of integration.)

The alienation of large segments of the public from city government is not new. But the absence of traditional reform-oriented civic groups in the educational arena is certainly significant. Several recent studies by educators seem to substantiate this as a general trend. As for parents associations, all the studies which have considered their specific role agree that they serve to reinforce official policy and rarely raise meaningful policy alternatives. Their concern, particularly in the larger cities, is channeled to local school problems and their impact on central school policymaking is negligible.[12] In all, the total effect, certainly in large cities, is a more or less complete internalization of school politics.

School Institutions and Change

Since the 1930's there has been no serious reevaluation of the role of the board of education as a political institution and only minor adjustments in the thinking about how a board should be constituted.[13] In part, this situation reflects only another aspect of the isolation of the school system — in this case, from the critical analysis of social scientists. From the limited data available on the functioning of school boards in large cities, it seems clear that there has been an evident decline in the participation of the board in the policy process. The Pois study of the Chicago school board provides sensitive insights into the reasons for the decline.[14] It is relevant that in New York City and Chicago, boards of education which were appointed by the mayor were abolished and replaced by boards chosen by civic selection panels. This has resulted in a diminished role in school policy for the mayor at least. But whether or not the board is elected or appointed appears to make little difference in the general tendency for boards to remove themselves from policymaking — and, at the same time, from the public. In one large city the board held its public hearings in a room that accommodated six outsiders.[15] Pois has noted the determination of the Chicago board not to hold its hearings in local districts.[16] It is true that one analyst, Gross, has noted that the superintendents of large cities tend to complain about their boards of education as being a "bad blockage" in policy.[17] However, this complaint may not signify direct participation on the part of the board so much as less acceptance by the superintendent of board "interference." In contrast to the Gross study and in support of the thesis advanced here, Bowman found that in the larger cities, boards generally agreed that the policymaking role belonged to the superintendent.[18]

The declining role in the policy process appears to be related to the professionalization of the school bureaucracy and to the feeling, which pervades school boards, that its members are not competent to make certain judgments. In any case, school boards are rarely innovative and usually are unwilling to make decisions that might create controversy in the community. (It may well be that the structure of school boards should be changed so as to permit them a more responsible role in educational policymaking.)

It is also possible to draw some general conclusions regarding school superintendents in large cities. A recent article argued that such superintendents had a relatively short professional life span.[19] The reasons given were the superintendent's inability to choose his own staff, the miasma of administrative detail, and the highly volatile political circumstance in large cities. In regard to the question of politics, however, two superintendents removed by their boards, in New York City and Chicago, were removed by boards appointed by the selection-panel procedure — that is, nonpolitical appointees. Table 7 indicates that in point of fact there is a considerable difference in the average tenure of superintendents in larger cities, with the data suggesting that superintendents appointed by *elected* boards remain in office for a longer period of time. Moreover, in cities where the board is elected, the selection of "outsiders" for the office of superintendent is more common.

It has been generally assumed that large cities are against outside appointments.[20] Actually the tendency to appoint a superintendent from the outside indicates something important about the operation of the school system, its willingness to accept change. There is no clear pattern as to which systems are more inclined to make outside appointments. Table 7 suggests, however, that size alone is not the most important variable. But there is some correlation in large cities between the acceptance of outsiders and appointed boards. Perhaps the appointed board is less concerned with keeping things as quiet as possible, since its members do not have to face reelection. The willingness of the Chicago and New York City boards to face public criticism for removing a superintendent might be explained the same way. Although the pressure to stay inside the system in the appointment of the superintendent is universal, actually doing so may be less prevalent in education than in other functional areas, given its relatively strong and well-developed professional ties. (For the same reason, boards of education in smaller communities may also be less likely to challenge their superintendent.)

TABLE 7

SCHOOL SUPERINTENDENTS, 1900 TO 1964

City	Insider	Outsider	Method of Selection	Average Term, 1900-64 (in years)
Baltimore	4	4	Mayor and Council	8
Boston	9	2	Elected	5.8
Buffalo*	2	2	Mayor and Council	12
Chicago	5	4	Mayor	7.8
Cleveland	6	4	Elected	6.4
Detroit	3	2	Elected	12.8
Houston*	2	2	Elected	10
Los Angeles	7	3	Elected	6.4
Milwaukee	3	3	Elected	10.6
New York	5	2	Mayor	9.1
Philadelphia	5	4	County Judges	7.8
Pittsburgh	3	5	County Judges	8
San Francisco	3	4	Mayor	9.1
Saint Louis	6	1	Elected	9.1

*Superintendent appointed as of 1917 in Buffalo, 1923 in Houston.
Source: Joseph M. Cronin, The Board of Education in Great Cities (doctoral dissertation, Stanford University, 1965).

Further, the merit system in larger cities and the increasingly routinized procedures for examining and promoting school administrators also serves to close off nonprofessional participants from school policy. Thus, political parties have virtually no role in school affairs. As a group, they have even been removed — or have removed themselves — from the desegregation issue. [21]

The elimination of public nonprofessional participants from school policy-making, whatever the cause or however beneficial the results in some instances, leaves a vacuum in leadership and diminishes, almost to the vanishing point, competition and interest. If the test of viability in a political system is the ability to convert demands into policies, the sharp tendencies toward preservation of the *status quo* in city school systems in the face of the changing composition of the contemporary metropolis is a matter of serious concern. If the lack of ability to meet changing needs is related to the closed nature of the system, as seems to be the case in the area of education, then it is clear that the base of participation must be broadened.

There are those who would distinguish technical decisions from public decisions and thus rationalize the closed system of participation in school policy. However, if one regards the presentation of policy alternatives as a basic element in sounder decision making, the distinction becomes irrelevant, and the intrinsic importance of nonprofessional participation (in all areas of decision making) becomes clear.

Expanding Participation

Any effort to change the school system and expand civic participation must face the concentration of power in the professional bureaucracy and the resistance by the bureaucracy to any plan that would erode its power. Thus, any plan for change must have as its first objective the diminution of bureaucratic power. Meaningful plans for the reorganization of large city school systems must embody a formula for the decentralization of bureaucratic authority and the expansion of outside nonprofessional influences. Reorganization should also serve the purpose of maximizing public involvement in the schools, and of stimulating the mayor, other officials, civic groups, and a larger public to play more active roles in educational policy. Greater reliance on more local involvement through decentralization is the most natural approach to such a reorganization.

All of the vested interests in school politics oppose decentralization. This is true not only for the school supervisory staff and for teachers organizations but also for the lay members of the boards of education and even for the established education interest groups. Throughout the administrative hierarchy of the school system, only the superintendent of schools might clearly see his interests identified with decentralization; he alone could possibly maximize his authority over many small blocs of power more readily than he can over the few large power blocs that now exist. But other high-level administrators at central headquarters derive their power from the weight of hierarchical responsibilities. Even district superintendents, who would have enhanced authority under a decentralization plan, conceivably may prefer the *status quo;* they may see any new authority negated by the pressure of parent and other local groups that would be channeled locally.

The city board of education, similarly, will find its power diminished by the existence of strong local school boards. Teachers organizations prefer to negotiate their demands centrally, backed by the weight of the entire teaching force of a city's schools. A union would naturally view decentralization as a threat to its solidified power. Further, the unions inevitably would oppose an arrangement flexible enough to permit district variation in such areas as teaching responsibilities, class size, and basis for advancement.

The forces that favor the strong central school structure prevail outside the system as well as inside. Major civic groups with an interest in education are structured in a centralized fashion. Their major impact and avenues of influence are city-wide, not local. Similarly, civil rights groups have power city-wide and might fear a decentralized integration policy.

The most pressing and immediate problems of large city school systems are related to the changing character of city populations. The response to such change is usually a tendency to support plans for greater integration or for consolidation of city and suburban schools under a metropolitan school district, although no such consolidations have taken place. The purpose of such districts would be to alleviate financial inequities and provide a realistic basis for achieving racial integration. Certainly the financial burden of city schools would be abetted by such an arrangement. In New York, any plan for consolidation would have to be promulgated under state law and could only be achieved if encouragement was provided through the state-aid formula.

The likelihood of achieving metropolitan school districts in the foreseeable future is doubtful. Nevertheless, any plan for decentralization should provide a viable means for future consolidation by maintaining those central facilities and operations that could be readily consolidated.

Beyond the need to mobilize the support of powerful city groups, other additional difficulties beset plans to decentralize. Determining district lines and exactly which functions are to be assigned to a central and which to a local facility are substantial tasks. It is difficult to establish the appropriate dimensions for a district that at once is large enough to be powerful, small enough to be "local," different enough to break up existing power blocs, and, finally, a size that makes sense in the terms of the city. In addition to all this, working out viable district lines in cities with changing populations poses great problems. Equally difficult is the matter of creating a workable balance between localized and centralized functions that will produce increased participation, adaptability to local needs, and economies of scale, and will not clash with established political-fiscal machinery nor with established concepts of central control.

Possible Approaches to Decentralization

With these difficulties in mind, it is still possible to outline several approaches to decentralizing the school system in New York City. Moving from very small local units to large political divisions, the plans are as follows:

1. *Developing Educational Parks* — The educational park has been advanced as a new approach to a complex of problems. A park can afford to support extensive and expensive services. It offers at least a partial solution to segregation. It provides a basis for the flexibility essential to schools adapting to rapidly changing social needs.

The flexibility inherent in an educational park would require that the persons responsible for administering it be given a good deal of discretion. Therefore, to have a successful park, much authority would need to be decentralized to that level. While certain services and responsibilities would necessarily remain centralized, the radical nature of the proposed educational complex could fundamentally alter the policy process of education in the city.

2. *Local School Boards* — Another possible approach to reorganization involves the creation or strengthening of local school boards and providing them with significant decision-making powers over educational policy. School boards could be elected by nonpartisan vote to stimulate local participation in school affairs and encourage voter support for school programs.

Under such an arrangement, city-wide coordination might be assured by a central city school board which would continue to be appointed by the mayor for its regular task of defining basic educational objectives and policies. A small central school staff then could service the city-wide board and carry out school programs in the areas of planning, budget, curriculum research, accounting, purchasing, and personnel.

3. *Decentralizing Operations into City School Districts* — A third approach lies in establishing fewer school districts. A reorganization into approximately 15 to 20 districts might achieve maximum decentralization while maintaining

districts of sufficient size to provide for economic local administration. Each of the districts could be fiscally dependent on the city, and might be governed by local school boards appointed by the mayor from a list submitted by a local screening panel.

City funds could be appropriated to each district on a formula basis. Within the lump-sum appropriations, each district board could then have complete discretion in budget making and budget administration.

A central school advisory council and central school staff could continue to carry out centralized functions justified by economies of scale.

4. *Establishing Several Larger-Area School Districts* — Separate "area" school districts, fiscally dependent on the city government, might be established in place of the present single city-wide district. Each district might be governed by a separate board of education. The city could appropriate lump-sum a- mounts to each district determined on a formula basis.

Under this arrangement, a city-wide council might assume a coordinating function and, with a city school administrator appointed by the mayor, over- see and be responsible for defining city-wide school policies and minimum standards. A central planning advisory staff would operate centrally estab- lished, city-wide school programs for functions justified by demonstrated economies of scale.

The results of this study indicate that only minor procedural changes can be expected from the present educational system given the distribution of power within it. This power can be redistributed only through a thorough reorganization that will dislodge the central headquarters staff from its al- most complete control of policy. All of the above reorganization plans, there- fore, embody the principle of decentralization. Decentralization alone cannot create broader participation, but it can encourage participation through mak- ing the decision process more visible and by increasing competition among the participants. Additional mechanisms must be developed to stimulate greater involvement by the mayor, a diverse body of interest groups (professional and nonprofessional alike), and teachers and citizens concerned with broad as- pects of educational policy. Such changes can only be achieved if the school system's ties to the community are more immediate and more direct.

CHAPTER IX

Epilogue: A Plan for New York City

Five Borough School Districts

This chapter proposes the creation of borough school districts in New York City to shift major power from the city to the borough. Such a change provides avenues of expression for local groups; and with the existence of natural interborough rivalries, it encourages competition and change.

In brief, the plan proposes five borough school districts, each of which would be considered separate under state law. Each borough would have a school committee and its own superintendent of schools. The city's functions include overall responsibilities for long-range planning and for providing technical assistance. The city will have, as well, a certain amount of overall political and fiscal leverage to implement a role that is broadly coordinative. City-wide coordination would rest with a city school commissioner and a city board of education.

The plan provides for close cooperation with the municipal colleges, and, in general, opens the school system to new interests and new leadership.

Financing Five Borough School Districts

State aid for school districts in New York State takes into account the ability of the local district to finance its schools through property taxation. The device used is an aid ratio that determines the state share of total approved operating expenses. The aid ratio for each school district varies depending upon the relation to the state-wide average of the full value of taxable real property in the district. However, every district, regardless of wealth, receives a minimum amount of aid; districts which receive this minimum are called flat-grant districts.

New York City receives far less aid than it would if state aid was computed on a county-by-county basis, considering each county, or borough, a separate district. New York City, as a single unit for state aid purposes, is a flat-grant district because the concentration of great wealth in Manhattan compensates for the relatively low property values in the other boroughs. If aid was determined on a borough-by-borough basis (see Table 8), Manhattan and Queens would be flat-grant districts, the aid ratio for Richmond would rise slightly — and the aid ratios for Brooklyn and the Bronx would rise to over 60 per cent. More than half of the city's pupil population resides in these latter two boroughs.

TABLE 8

EFFECT OF SEPARATE BOROUGH COMPUTATIONS ON
STATE AID RATIOS FOR NEW YORK CITY

Borough	Pupils in WADA[a] 1963-64	Aid Ratio by Borough	Aid Ratio for State Aid Purposes
Manhattan	177,140	— b	36.0[c]
Bronx	190,728	64.6	64.6
Brooklyn	379,796	60.3	60.3
Queens	240,464	25.7	36.0[c]
Richmond	35,850	39.5	39.5
City-wide	1,023,978	34.1[c]	N/A

[a] *WADA - Weighted Average Daily Attendance.*
[b] *Negative aid ratio of −42.7 per cent.*
[c] *Minimum aid of 36.0 per cent.*
Source: Special Study of Bureau of School Financial Aid, *Board of Education, December 16, 1964.*

On such a borough-by-borough basis, estimates indicate that the city would receive about $100-million more in state aid per year than it currently receives. The state aid thus received could become part of the total New York City expense budget appropriation for education. The city, in turn, would provide each borough school district with a lump-sum appropriation, determined on a formula basis weighted for enrollment per grade and various handicap factors (e.g., frequency of reading retardation, emotional disturbance, physical handicaps among the pupil population). The precise formula would be developed by the city board of education. The borough school district would determine how its funds were to be used.

The city should require that each borough use a performance budget and exercise control over its appropriations through an operations review, conducted by the city administrator's office. (As already noted, one of the obvious shortcomings in the present structure is the lack of program orientation in budgeting, and the fact that review of performance is almost nonexistent.)

The city school commissioner should also have available a substantial fund to award grants for imaginative proposals. In effect, the large city should be viewed as a granting agency in several functional areas. Grants could be made to encourage a wide range of experimental programs (e.g., team teaching, curriculum development, new methods of structuring classes), and conceivably could be awarded to the borough school district, or to lesser units, including individual schools, teachers, and possibly parent or other groups. The awarding of grants should spur competition, innovation, and community involvement in the school. This procedure would increase the role of the mayor and the city in the development of school policy. Imaginative programs and experimentation would be supported by city funds.

As a further stimulus to community involvement, it might be possible to develop procedures to permit districts to levy additional taxes for facilities beyond those obtained with expense budget and grant-award funds. This would give community groups an opportunity to participate more directly in framing school policy, and more important, permit them the opportunity of evaluating alternatives.

The City-Wide Function

Within the broadly coordinating role of the city, there would be several offices and functions. The mayor would appoint the city school commissioner, who would head a small staff and serve as executive officer to the city board of education. The city school commissioner would also function as chairman of the city school council, composed of the five borough superintendents of schools. In addition to the city school council, the borough systems would be coordinated in a city-wide, comprehensive, long-range plan for education.

The New York City Board of Education

In the plan proposed here, the board of education is envisioned as a prestigious body, fashioned after the State Board of Regents. Its major role would be to develop a long-range plan for the schools in New York City. Its plan should concentrate on the public schools, but, as the Regents' plan, might encompass the private schools as well. It also should concern itself with higher education and could provide a much-needed coordinating function between the schools and the colleges. The board may require reports from the borough school committees, necessarily would require individual master plans, and may issue its own reports, as the Regents have done.

The board, composed of perhaps 14 members, should be appointed in a manner to insure high quality and prestige, broad representation, political astuteness, and the cooperation of the colleges and schools. Thus, one member would be the Chancellor of the City University, three would be appointed by the mayor, two by the City Council, and three by a selection panel. The chairmen of the borough school committees would comprise the remainder.

The Mayor

The proposed structure, in defining a long-range planning and coordinating city-wide function, heightens the mayor's role in broad educational policy-making. The ability of the mayor to influence educational policy is maximized by the provisions for: (1) mayoral appointment of the city school commission; (2) mayoral appointment of three members of the city board of education; and (3) mayoral review and comment on the long-range plan for education in New York City.

One of the most obvious deficiencies in the present education structure has been the weakened position of the mayor as an initiator of educational policy. Although borough systems might appear to further detract from the mayor's role, appropriate mechanisms can be provided to encourage his participation on a meaningful level. The grant program offers the opportunity to expand his leadership role in supporting new programs. The expanded review function of the mayor guarantees constant city-wide evaluation of the borough school system.

The City Commissioner of Schools

The key city-wide post would be the commissioner of schools. Appointed by the mayor for a four-year term, the commissioner would serve as the mayor's chief adviser on education, be the executive officer of the board of education, and have no line function. He would direct a small staff which would conduct ongoing research in areas such as curriculum and school construction. The research handled by a borough system would necessarily — and usefully — be molded by the exigencies of day-to-day operations. Having a central research function as well, would provide for equally important long-term inquiry.

The commissioner's staff would be able to provide technical assistance to the borough systems, such as advising them on matters of master planning and recruitment of teachers, and providing in-service training programs.

The commissioner's office would coordinate state and federal aid, administer the grant program, and conduct city-wide negotiations with the teachers union.

The City School Council

The city school council would be composed of the superintendents of schools of each of the five borough systems and the city school commissioner, who would be its chairman. The council would have no legal authority, but would meet periodically and provide opportunities for the exchange of information and for cooperation and coordination on a professional level.

Divided Functions

Under the proposed plan, some functions would be apportioned between the city and the borough. They include: (1) recruitment, personnel, standards, and union negotiations; (2) school construction and site selection; and (3) long-range planning.

City-wide standards for teachers would be minimal: a teacher should have New York State certification and should satisfy requirements set by the department of health. Beyond these standards, a borough would have the discretion to recruit teachers and set up examinations or other selection procedures deemed useful. The city school commissioner, however, could provide relevant technical assistance or a central nationwide recruiting service if requested.

The commissioner of schools would negotiate a basic city-wide contract with the United Federation of Teachers to determine: (1) the minimum and maximum steps on a salary scale; (2) pension and welfare benefits; and (3) minimum tenure standards for teachers (e.g., not to be conferred before three-years service nor after seven years). The borough system would define its own policy within these determinations. All other arrangements — provisions affecting administrative personnel, class size, teaching assignments and hours, salary steps between the minimum and maximum — would be negotiated at the borough level.

Construction and site selection should be determined in each borough. However, for adequate city-wide coordination it would be necessary to follow the procedures set by the City Planning Commission.

Long-range planning would be a function at both levels. The boroughs would have to develop master plans to submit to the central board. The board, in turn, would have to consider and evaluate the plans and incorporate them into an overall city-wide plan.

The Borough System

Under the reorganized structure, the power now lodged at Board of Education headquarters would be shifted to the borough district. Each borough would have a borough school committee that would appoint a borough superintendent of schools.

Appointment of the School Committee

To insure a responsive policymaking body, the appointments to the borough committee should reflect the gamut of interests and needs in the borough. This study recommends a five-member committee composed as follows: one to be chosen by the borough president; one the president of a municipal college located in the borough; and three to be chosen by a broadly-based selection panel.

The nomination by the borough president should provide the board with a member who has political acumen and political leverage. The presence of a municipal college president would provide an academic point of view, and significantly should stimulate much needed school-university cooperation. If there is more than one municipal college in the borough, the Chancellor of the City University should determine a rotation schedule for the college presidents.

Having the majority of the members of the school committee appointed by the selection panel will maximize community involvement. The panel of say 20 members should be elected at a borough convention. The borough convention should be broadly representative, with delegates from parent associations, civic orgaizations and church groups, and the poverty-area conventions. The borough convention conceivably could develop into an active association, with the power base and influence to demand a responsive school committee.

The Functions of the Borough School System

The role of the school committee would be to select a superintendent of schools, formulate policy, and develop a master plan to be submitted to the city board.

The school committee and the superintendent would be charged with defining the organizational structure of the new borough district. Three areas should be retained by the committee and the superintendent as centralized functions: (1) zoning — to insure integration; (2) purchase — to insure economies of scale; and (3) construction — to insure economies of scale and central planning.

Beyond these centralized functions, it is hoped that each borough system would develop an imaginative and flexible pattern of organization, guarding against the overcentralization and rigidity that have stifled the present system. The establishment of parent-teacher committees to operate schools, plan budgets, and set curriculum should not be overlooked.

Ideally, "conventional wisdom" would be discarded in structuring the new systems. For example, the administrative leadership of a school might rest not with a principal, but with a master teacher whose main concern is the classroom and whose purely administrative tasks are assumed by an administrative assistant — who need not necessarily be a teacher. In fact, the whole assumption that school administrators ought to be teachers should be challenged. Currently, the road to advancement in the school system is from teaching to administration, and there is no prestige attached to remaining a teacher. New teaching positions (e.g., master teacher, team leader) could be developed and recognition assured through higher salaries.

The existence of five borough districts would enhance the possibility of infusing new leadership into the schools. One borough might select a superintendent from outside New York City. Another might choose as superintendent or as a high official in the system a person from outside the field of education. The superintendent's position could be strengthened by permitting him to select his own top staff.

Under this plan, varying amounts of authority could be decentralized to the local level, while varying types of experiments in community involvement could be tried. Local school boards could be elected and individual schools could receive lump-sum budgets. Campus schools could be increased, and close cooperation with the college is likely to lead to innumerable new approaches in all areas of education.

New concepts in building, in programs, and in teaching personnel could be encouraged under flexible arrangements. The proximity of the boroughs and the city school council would insure the exchange of information about the success of experiments. In fundamentally reorganizing the current rigid structure, the proposal for five borough systems is replete with possibilities for dramatic, revitalizing change.

APPENDIX A
Selected Tables
Table I

PERCENTAGE DISTRIBUTION OF PUBLIC SCHOOL ENROLLMENTS BY ETHNIC GROUP, SCHOOL LEVEL, AND BOROUGH: NEW YORK CITY, 1957-58 AND 1964-65

Area and Ethnic Group	All Schools 1964-5	1957-8	Elementary 1964-5	1957-8	Junior High 1964-5	1957-8	Academic High 1964-5	1957-8	Vocational High 1964-5	1957-8
New York City										
Negro	27.3	18.2	30.1	20.5	28.0	18.9	18.2	9.3	28.6	23.6
Puerto Rican	18.2	13.5	20.7	15.3	18.7	16.1	8.9	4.6	24.2	20.4
Other	54.5	68.3	49.2	64.2	53.3	65.0	72.9	86.1	47.2	56.0
Bronx										
Negro	26.9	15.6	28.6	17.1	26.7	14.7	20.9	9.5	29.3	25.8
Puerto Rican	30.6	19.8	34.2	22.6	30.4	21.2	15.9	6.5	46.2	35.9
Other	42.5	64.6	37.2	60.3	42.9	64.1	63.2	84.0	24.5	38.3
Brooklyn										
Negro	29.5	17.5	33.3	21.0	30.5	16.7	16.8	7.4	27.8	24.0
Puerto Rican	16.9	10.2	19.9	12.2	16.9	11.5	6.5	2.4	20.6	16.0
Other	53.6	72.3	46.8	66.8	52.6	71.8	76.7	90.2	51.6	60.0
Manhattan										
Negro	38.9	32.7	41.2	35.7	39.2	33.7	33.9	24.3	31.3	24.8
Puerto Rican	32.6	30.4	36.0	33.6	34.2	34.0	22.2	16.9	26.5	24.0
Other	28.5	36.9	22.8	30.7	26.6	32.3	43.9	58.8	42.2	51.2
Queens										
Negro	18.9	10.9	21.5	12.4	19.2	12.5	11.9	5.1	21.9	16.8
Puerto Rican	2.1	1.4	2.0	1.7	2.1	1.5	1.4	0.7	9.0	2.8
Other	79.0	87.7	76.5	85.9	78.7	86.0	86.7	94.2	69.1	80.4
Richmond										
Negro	8.1	6.2	8.9	7.1	9.7	—	4.6	2.6	11.2	12.0
Puerto Rican	2.1	1.4	2.1	1.7	2.5	—	1.6	0.6	4.5	1.8
Other	89.8	92.4	89.0	91.2	87.8	—	93.8	96.8	84.3	86.2

Sources: Derived from unpublished tabulations of Special Census of School Population, January 15, 1965, supplied by Board of Education, City of New York; and Board of Education, City of New York, News Bureau Release, N-151-63/64, January 6, 1964 (mimeographed); and from Sheldon and Glazier, Pupils and Schools in New York City, p. 117.

Table II

CHANGE IN ENROLLMENTS IN PUBLIC AND NONPUBLIC SCHOOLS
BY SCHOOL LEVEL: NEW YORK CITY, 1950 TO 1960

(NUMBERS IN THOUSANDS)

School Level and Type	Enrollment 1960	Enrollment 1950	Change 1950 to 1960 Number	Change 1950 to 1960 Per Cent
All Levels (K-12)[a]	1,396	1,179	217	18.4
Public	987	879	108	12.3
Nonpublic	409	300	109	36.3
Kindergarten	89	64	25	39.1
Public	75	54	21	38.9
Nonpublic	14	10	4	40.0
Elementary (1-8)	926	805	121	15.0
Public	607	565	42	7.4
Nonpublic	319	240	79	32.9
High School	366	306	60	19.6
Public	290	256	34	13.3
Nonpublic	76	50	26	52.0

[a] *Includes figures for handicapped pupils in public schools who were not under grade classification. These numbered about 4,000 in 1950, and 16,000 in 1960.*

Sources: Derived from Board of Education, City of New York, Sixty-Third Annual Report of the Super-intendent of Schools, Statistical Section, School Year 1960-61, Tables 21-23; Fifty-Seventh Annual Report..., School Year 1954-55, Table 36.

Table III

ENROLLMENTS IN NONPUBLIC SCHOOLS AS PER CENT OF
TOTAL ENROLLMENTS BY SCHOOL LEVEL:
NEW YORK CITY, 1950 TO 1962

School Level	1950	1955	1957	1960	1962
All Levels	25.4	28.8	29.0	29.3	28.7
Below High School (K-8)	28.8	32.1	32.5	32.8	31.8
Kindergarten	15.6	16.7	16.0	15.7	14.4
Elementary (1-8)	29.8	33.5	34.0	34.5	33.6
High School (1-12)	16.3	20.2	20.2	20.5	21.4

Sources: Derived from Board of Education, City of New York, Sixty-Fifth Annual Report of the Superintendent of Schools, Statistical Section; School Year 1962-63, Tables 46-49; Sixty-Third Annual Report..., School Year 1960-61, Tables 21-23; Sixtieth Annual Report..., School Year 1957-58, Tables 21,22, 24; Fifty-Seventh Annual Report..., School Year 1954-55, Table 36.

Table IV

DAY SCHOOL INSTRUCTION: NUMBER OF POSITIONS AND COSTS FOR TEACHERS AND OTHER PERSONNEL 1954-55 AND 1964-65

	1954-55		1964-65		Amount of Increase		Percentage Increase	
	No. of Positions	Cost	No. of Positions	Cost	No. of Positions	Cost	No. of Positions	Cost
Elementary								
Teachers	17,996	$102,978,319	21,939	$175,253,307	3,943	$ 72,274,988	21.9	70.2
Other	1,707	10,576,780	2,472	24,575,371	765	13,988,591	44.8	132.4
Sub-total	19,703	$113,555,099	24,411	$199,828,678	4,708	$ 86,273,579	23.9	76.0
Junior High								
Teachers	5,639	$ 30,292,577	10,942	$ 87,159,495	5,303	$ 56,866,918	94.0	187.7
Other	589	3,632,418	1,233	12,353,094	644	8,720,676	109.3	240.1
Sub-total	6,228	$ 33,924,995	12,175	$ 99,512,589	5,947	$ 65,587,594	95.5	193.3
Academic High								
Teachers	5,651	$ 37,346,802	8,105	$ 76,060,879	2,454	$ 38,714,077	43.4	103.7
Other	1,294	8,124,989	1,474	15,173,921	180	7,048,932	13.9	86.8
Sub-total	6,945	$ 45,471,791	9,579	$ 91,234,800	2,634	$ 45,763,009	37.9	100.6
Vocational High								
Teachers	2,427	$ 14,568,890	2,439	$ 23,296,470	12	$ 8,727,580	4.5	60.0
Other	378	2,422,504	362	3,848,029	−16	1,425,525	−4.2	58.8
Sub-total	2,805	$ 16,991,394	2,801	$ 27,144,499	− 4	$ 10,153,105	−0.1	59.8
Special Schools and Classes								
Teachers	1,862	$ 10,500,902	2,636	$ 23,256,884	774	$ 12,755,982	41.6	121.5
Other	53	320,826	102	959,063	49	638,237	92.5	199.0
Sub-total	1,915	$ 10,821,728	2,738	$ 24,215,947	823	$ 13,394,219	43.0	123.8
Shop Maintenance	26	$ 114,425	6	$ 39,180	−20	$ −75,245	—	—
TOTAL	37,622	$220,879,432	51,710	$441,975,693	14,088	$221,096,261	37.4	100.1

Source: Board of Education, City School District of the City of New York, Budgets for Fiscal Years 1954-55 and 1964-65.

Table V

DAY SCHOOL INSTRUCTION: NUMBER OF POSITIONS AND COST

1954-55 AND 1964-65

Position	1954-55		1964-65		Increase	
	Number	Cost	Number	Cost	Number	Cost
Principals	789	$ 7,310,287	865	$ 13,444,405	76	$ 6,134,118
Assistant Principals [a]	668	5,031,910	1,386	17,461,058	718	12,429,148
Chairman of Departments	634	4,935,795	740	9,701,967	106	4,766,172
Teachers [b]	33,575	195,687,490	46,061	385,027,035	12,486	189,339,545
Laboratory Assistants	192	840,070	290	1,874,678	98	1,034,608
School Secretaries	1,669	6,692,728	2,338	14,307,225	669	7,614,497
Shower Room Attendants	57	207,927	24	120,145	−33	−87,782
Placement and Investigation Assistants	12	58,800	0	0	−12	−58,800
Shop Maintenance Men	26	114,425	6	39,180	−20	−75,245
TOTAL	37,622	$220,879,432	51,710	$441,975,693	14,108	$221,096,261

[a] Administrative Assistants are listed under Assistant Principals. High Schools have Administrative Assistants, not Assistant Principals. In 1964-65 there were 7 such positions, 5 in Academic High Schools and 2 in Vocational High Schools.

[b] Includes Library Assistants.

Source: Board of Education, City School District of the City of New York, Budgets for the Fiscal Years 1954-55 and 1964-65.

Table VI

**NUMBER OF POSITIONS AND COST OF SALARIES
IN ELEMENTARY SCHOOLS
1954-55 AND 1964-65**

Position	1954-55		1964-65	
	Number	*Cost*	*Number*	*Cost*
Principals	558	$ 4,820,514	593	$ 8,874,566
Assistants to Principals	332	2,506,307	688	8,593,895
Teachers:[a]				
Regular, grades 1-8[b]	16,230	93,444,477	19,888	158,892,002
Kindergarten	1,476	7,768,758	1,961	15,591,231
Industrial Arts	134	781,493	29	266,691
Home Economics	138	744,331	46	365,883
Swimming	18	116,860	15	137,500
Sub-Total	*17,996*	*$102,855,919*	*21,939*	*$175,253,307*
School Secretaries	807	$ 3,213,297	1,190	$ 7,102,015
Shower Room Attendants	*10*	*36,662*	*1*	*4,895*
TOTAL	*19,703*	*$113,555,099*	*24,411*	*$199,828,678*

[a] *Teachers of classes for handicapped children are listed under Special Schools and Classes in the 1954-55 Budget. In the 1964-65 Budget, Teachers of Special Classes for handicapped children in Elementary Schools are listed under Elementary Schools. Teachers of Speech are listed under Elementary Schools in the 1954-55 Budget and under Teaching-Speech Improvement, in the 1964-65 Budget. For purposes of comparison they are listed under Special Schools, Special Classes, and Other in these tables.*

[b] *Other Teaching Positions (not classroom teachers but special teachers for remedial reading, library, art, science, music, etc.) are included in Regular Teachers.*

Source: Board of Education, City School District of the City of New York, Budgets for the Fiscal Years 1954-55 and 1964-65.

Table VII

**NUMBER OF POSITIONS AND COST OF SALARIES
IN JUNIOR HIGH SCHOOLS
1954-55 AND 1964-65**

Position	1954-55		1964-65	
	Number	Cost	Number	Cost
Principals	102	$ 1,013,329	138	$ 2,231,014
Assistant Principals	217	1,519,491	539	6,792,610
Teachers:[a]				
Regular	4,846	26,008,858	9,448	74,372,425
Home Economics	344	1,727,207	622	5,265,406
Industrial Arts	438	2,138,340	720	6,225,658
Swimming	11	61,320	13	108,700
Library	—	—	139	1,187,306
Sub-Total	5,639	$ 30,292,577	10,942	$ 98,159,495
Laboratory Assistants	—	—	67	391,448
Shower Room Attendants	21	75,964	21	103,670
School Secretaries	249	951,634	468	2,834,352
TOTAL	6,228	$ 33,924,995	12,175	$ 99,512,589

[a] *In the 1954-55 Budget, Teachers of handicapped children are listed under Special Schools and Special Classes. In the 1964-65 Budget, Teachers of Special Classes for handicapped are distributed among the regular school divisions in which they are located. For purposes of comparison, they are listed under Special Schools and Classes in these tables.*

Source: Board of Education, City School District of the City of New York, Budgets for the Fiscal Years 1954-55 and 1964-65.

Table VIII

NUMBER OF POSITIONS AND COST IN ACADEMIC HIGH SCHOOLS
1954-55 AND 1964-65

Position	1954-55		1964-65	
	Number	Cost	Number	Cost
Principals	54	$ 716,507	59	$ 1,150,418
Administrative Assistants	89	698,116	122	1,590,437
Chairman of Departments	509	3,991,667	611	8,006,584
Teachers:				
Regular	5,406	36,004,129	7,784	73,046,227
Handicapped[a]	—	—	27	254,093
C.R.M.D.[b]	—	—	45	450,752
Library	141	712,409	180	1,684,599
Library Assistants	32	158,522	5	38,100
Swimming	72	471,742	64	587,108
Sub-Total	5,651	$ 37,346,802	8,105	$ 76,060,879
Laboratory Assistants	162	710,656	189	1,253,983
Shower Room Attendants	15	55,177	2	11,580
Placement and Investigating Assistants	10	49,000	—	—
School Secretaries	455	1,903,866	491	3,160,919
TOTAL	6,945	$ 45,471,791	9,579	$191,234,800

[a] *Teachers of Classes for Deaf, Blind, Sight Conservation, Health Conservation.*

[b] *Teachers of Classes for Children with Retarded Mental Development.*

Source: Board of Education, City School District of the City of New York, Budgets for the Fiscal Years 1954-55 and 1964-65.

Table IX

NUMBER OF POSITIONS AND COST IN VOCATIONAL HIGH SCHOOLS
1954-55 AND 1964-65

Position	1954-55		1964-65	
	Number	Cost	Number	Cost
Principals and Others in Charge	51	$ 567,702	33	$ 622,164
Assistants to Principals	27	211,788	31	407,420
Chairman of Departments	125	944,128	129	1,695,383
Teachers:				
Regular	2,371	14,275,771	2,377	22,749,493
Handicapped[a]	—	—	4	30,592
C.R.M.D.[b]	—	—	4	38,808
Library	45	230,147	49	435,412
Library Assistants	7	35,772	2	15,665
Swimming	4	27,200	3	26,500
Sub-Total	2,427	$ 14,568,890	2,439	$ 23,296,470
School Secretaries	132	519,548	135	893,815
Laboratory Assistants	30	129,414	34	229,247
Shower Room Attendants	11	40,124	—	—
Placement and Investigating Assistants	2	9,800	—	—
TOTAL	2,805	$ 16,991,394	2,801	$ 27,144,499

[a] *Teachers of Classes for Deaf and Health Conservation.*

[b] *Teachers of Classes for Children with Retarded Mental Development.*

Source: Board of Education, City School District of the City of New York, Budgets for the Fiscal Years 1954-55 and 1964-65.

Table X

**NUMBER OF POSITIONS AND COST FOR SPECIAL SCHOOLS,
SPECIAL CLASSES, AND SPECIAL TEACHERS
1954-55 AND 1964-65**

Position	1954-55		1964-65	
	Number	*Cost*	*Number*	*Cost*
Special Schools[a] and Classes[b]				
Principals	24	$ 192,235	42	$ 566,243
Assistants to Principals	3	24,208	6	76,696
Teachers:				
Special Schools[c]	1,512	8,765,634	885	8,019,121
Junior High	—	—	317	2,776,011
Elementary	—	—	—	—
Sub-Total	*1,539*	*$ 8,765,634*	*2,114*	*$ 18,552,257*
School Secretaries	26	104,383	54	316,124
TOTAL	*1,565*	*$ 9,086,460*	*2,216*	*$ 19,511,320*
Special Teachers				
Home Teachers for Physically Handicapped Children	237	1,180,778	328	3,164,191
Speech Improvement Teachers[d]	113	554,490	194	1,540,436
TOTAL	*350*	*$ 1,735,268*	*522*	*$ 4,704,627*
GRAND TOTAL	*1,915*	*$ 10,821,728*	*2,738*	*$ 24,215,947*

[a] *Special Schools:*

	1954-55	1964-65
Occupational Training Center for Mentally Retarded Children	*1*	*1*
School for the Deaf	*1*	*2*
"600" Schools	*14*	*29*
"400" Schools	*8*	*9*
Shelter School	*1*	*—*

[b] *Special Classes:*

Health Conservation — for children with orthopedic handicaps, cardiac diseases, and other physical limitations.
Sight Conservation — for children with limited vision.
Braille — for blind children.
C.R.M.D. — for children with retarded mental development.

[c] *In the 1954-55 Budget, teachers of Special Classes in elementary schools and junior high schools were listed under Special Schools and Classes. In the 1964-65 Budget these teachers are listed under the School Division in which they taught. For purposes of comparison, all teachers of Special Classes are listed above.*

[d] *In the 1954-55 Budget, Speech Improvement Teachers were listed under Elementary Schools. In the 1964-65 Budget, they were listed separately.*

Source: Board of Education, City School District of New York, Budgets for Fiscal Years 1954-55 and 1964-65.

Table XI

NON-EDUCATIONAL PERSONNEL: NUMBER OF POSITIONS AND COST, BY FUNCTION
1954-55 AND 1964-65

	1954-55		1964-65		Amount of Increase		Percentage Increase	
	Number	*Cost*	*Number*	*Cost*	*Number*	*Cost*	*Number*	*Cost*
School Lunch	20	$ 70,763	1,303	$12,848,845	1,283	$12,778,082	6,415	18,050
Plant Operation, Maintenance and Construction	1,940	22,347,011	2,753	47,399,439	813	25,052,428	42	112
Other	1,203	3,601,217	1,698	10,042,286	495	6,441,069	41	179
TOTAL	3,163	$26,018,991	5,754	$70,290,570	2,591	$44,271,579	82	170

Table XI   Source: Board of Education, City School District of the City of New York, Budgets for the Fiscal Years 1954-55 and 1964-65.

Table XII

DISTRIBUTION OF SPECIAL SERVICE TEACHERS (OTHER TEACHING POSITIONS) IN THE ELEMENTARY SCHOOLS 1954-55 AND 1964-65

	Number	
Positions	*1954-55*	*1964-65*
Teachers for Remedial Reading	143	932
Teachers Assigned to Special Areas (Art, Health Education, Music, and Science)		541
Teachers of Library		469
Coordinator and Auxiliary Teachers, Non-English Speaking Pupils	48	285
Higher Horizon Program		163
All Day Neighborhood Schools	42	99
First Grade Resource Teachers		35
Teachers on other Assignments	18	186
Coordinators, Teachers Training		17
Coordinators (Art, Health Education, Music, Science, Reading)	61	110[a]
TOTAL	*312*	*2,837*

[a] *Of the 110 coordinators, 26 are for reading and 84 for science, mathematics and health.*

Source: Board of Education, City School District of the City of New York, tentative Budget 1965-66. Fiscal year information for 1954-55 obtained from the Elementary School Division of the Board of Education.

Table XIII

**SALARIES OF SUPERVISORY AND ADMINISTRATIVE PERSONNEL
1954-55 AND 1964-65**

| Positions | Salaries | |
	1954-55	1964-65
Superintendent of Schools	$32,500	$40,000
Executive Deputy Superintendent	*	32,500
Deputy Superintendent	25,000	27,500
Associate Superintendent	16,250	25,095
Assistant Superintendent	13,950	21,550
Examiners, Board of Examiners	14,300	22,245
School Medical Director	9,500	18,560
Director, Bureau of Attendance	16,250	25,095
Director, Bureau of Child Guidance	15,600	22,255
Director, Other Bureaus[a]	8,900-13,450	15,635-19,160
Assistant Director, Bureau of Attendance	13,950	21,550
Assistant Director, Bureau of Child Guidance	13,450	19,360
Assistant Director, Other Bureaus	7,450-10,200	13,720-15,735
Assistant Administrative Director	6,900- 8,900	14,465-18,080
Supervisor	6,850- 7,450	11,780-12,925
Inspector	6,450- 6,450	9,280-15,235
Coordinator	*	13,400-14,000
Principal	6,100-13,450	13,910-20,045

*Position did not exist in 1954-55.

[a] Includes Division Supervising Attendance Officer.

Source: Board of Education, City School District of the City of New York, Budget for the Fiscal Years 1954-55 and 1964-65.

Table XIV

THE INCREASED COST OF EDUCATION AS A RESULT OF
COLLECTIVE BARGAINING WITH
THE UNITED FEDERATION OF TEACHERS
(IN MILLIONS)

	Resulting from 1963 Agreement[b]	Resulting from 1965 Agreement[c]			
		Total	1965-66	1966-67	1967-68
Teachers' salaries and benefits	20.7	44.7	18.8	24.2	1.7
Other salaries	5.5	13.4[a]	5.7[a]	7.2[b]	.5[a]
Pension costs	5.3	9.0	—	9.0	.1
Total effect on city budget	31.5	67.1	24.5	40.4	2.3
Currently available in Board of Education Budget	—	21.5	21.5	—	—
Additional amount required from the city	—	45.6	3.0	40.4	2.3
Nonsalary benefits and quality improvement	6.0	26.0[d]	—	—	—
TOTAL COST	37.5	93.1	—	—	—

[a] *Excludes resulting salary increases for instructional staff of Board of Higher Education. (Estimated at $7 million.)*

[b] *Data from* The New York Times, *September 19, 1963.*

[c] *Data from the Board of Education.*

[d] *Presumed to be financed from federal funds.*

Table XV

**REASONS FOR INCREASE IN BUDGETED EXPENDITURES
FOR TEACHERS' SALARIES
1954-55 AND 1964-65**

Reasons	Amount of Increase[a]	Per Cent of Total
Increase in salary rates	$102,243,600	54%
Increase in number of teachers for:		
Increased enrollment	$ 37,868,000	20
Increase in special services	20,827,400	11
Reduction in teaching periods	15,147,200	8
Reduction in class size	13,253,800	7
Sub-Total	$ 87,096,400	46%
TOTAL	$189,340,000	100%

[a] *Computations were based on estimated enrollment, numbers of authorized teaching positions, utilization of teacher time, changes in pupil-teacher ratios, and estimated class size.*

The District Superintendents

The following data represent the results of a field survey questionnaire administered to nine of the then (1966) 25 district superintendents. Each superintendent was interviewed for several hours. The sample was selected so as to include representative districts in each borough. The significant characteristics of each district are outlined in Table I. Background data for the superintendents are indicated in Table II. As a group, they are relatively old, eight of the nine have been in the system over 36 years. Almost all have served one to ten years in their present job. All but one were principals in New York City schools prior to their appointment as an assistant superintendent.

Questions were directed at determining the field superintendent's perceptions of his job as well as establishing his actual practices.

Most of the superintendents agreed that their jobs entailed some kind of supervision of the schools and personnel in their districts. A comparatively large number viewed their public relations role as especially significant. When asked more specifically for whom they were responsible, most agreed that the principals were their particular concern. Few indicated that the supervision of teachers was a primary responsibility. Follow-up questions on their contact with principals, however, revealed a surprising lack of contact, except in formal monthly meetings. Individual conferences with principals were rare, evaluation scanty, and services to principals limited. (See Table V.) Although the district superintendent can appoint principals in his district, only two had done so, and only one had rated a principal after appointment.

District superintendent relationships with teachers were even more narrow. Few techniques have been developed for working with the teachers or for supervising their work. The district superintendent is obviously not someone teachers call on for assistance. In terms of their role as liaison with headquarters few indicated a significant role for themselves in that area. (See Table VI.)

Although curriculum coordinators operate out of district superintendent's offices, even that function appeared to be one in which they had only narrow involvement. It was clear that only two of them were actually functioning as overseers of personnel and curriculum in their local school area. In addition, at least half of the respondents did not appear to be involved with policy on a local level, indicated by the recurrence of the number four or five in response to key questions. Three of those interviewed were participating to a very limited degree.

Assignment of special personnel was very circumscribed at the time of the questioning in 1966. Since that time, additional personnel has been assigned to the districts and presumably superintendents would now be active in this regard.

When asked about activities on a typical day, superintendents commonly noted visits to schools and group meetings with staff. Such visits, however, have little to do with review of teachers, principals, or curriculum. Finally, meetings with parents and outsiders are more common than meetings with principals or teachers. (See Table IV.)

Table I

DISTRICT SUPERINTENDENT QUESTIONNAIRE
DISTRICT CHARACTERISTICS, 1966

DS#	Location	Economic	% White	% Nonwhite
1	Brooklyn	Middle	*	*
2	Queens	Low-High	78	22
3	Brooklyn	Low	50	50
4	Manhattan	Low-Middle	25	75
5	Manhattan	Low-Middle	30	70
6	Bronx	Low	10	90
7	Richmond	Middle	90	10
8	Queens	Middle-High	*	*
9	Bronx	Middle-High	70	30

*Predominantly white; no percentages available.

Table II

DISTRICT SUPERINTENDENT QUESTIONNAIRE
NUMBER OF YEARS IN SYSTEM
AND PREVIOUS ASSIGNMENT
SAMPLE OF 9 DS, 1966

	Number of DS
Years in N.Y.C. School System	
30-35	1
36-40	7
41-45	1
Years in this position	
1-5	3
6-10	5
11-15	1
Previous Assignment	
Principal	8
Other within N.Y.C. education system	1

Table III

DISTRICT SUPERINTENDENT QUESTIONNAIRE
CONCEPTION OF DUTIES AND RESPONSIBILITIES
SAMPLE OF 9 DS, 1966

	Number of DS
Conception of Duties	
Improvement of education and instruction	5
Administrative and organizational	5
Public relations	4
Liaison with headquarters	1
General supervision of schools and personnel	6
Implementation of curriculum	3
Curriculum experimentation	1
Training of new principals	1
Guidance of principals	1
Observation of teachers	2
Evaluation of teachers	1
Conception of Area of Responsibility	
School administrators	1
Principals	7
Teachers	5
School staffs (other than professional)	3
Local school boards	1
Parent organizations	1

Table IV
DISTRICT SUPERINTENDENT QUESTIONNAIRE
ACTIVITIES ON A TYPICAL DAY
SAMPLE OF 8 DS, 1966

Activities on Typical Day	Number of DS
Visits schools	8
Group meetings with school personnel (supervisors, principals and assistant principals, teachers, counselors, and administrative staff)	6
Individual conferences with principals or teachers	2
Meetings with other persons or groups (excluding parents)	4
Meetings with parents (individually and groups)	4
Local school board meetings	2
Observation of probationary teachers	2
Reports to headquarters	2
Reorganization sheets	1
Conferences with own staff	3
Maintenance matters	1

Table V
DISTRICT SUPERINTENDENT QUESTIONNAIRE
DS RELATIONSHIPS AND MEETINGS WITH PRINCIPALS
SAMPLE OF 9 DS, 1966

Relationships	Number of DS
Supervises work	2
Committee meetings and conferences of principals	4
Committee meetings and conferences of assistant principals	1
Individual conferences	2
Evaluation of principals	2
Handles special problems concerning staff for principals	2
Handles special discipline problems for principals	1
Services principals through coordinator	1
Aids principal in implementing programs	1
Has special committees for various problems	1
Formal Meetings	
Once a month meetings	9
Committee meetings	6
Individual conferences for special problems	2
Meetings with assistant principals	3
Special meetings as need arises	5
Informal Meetings	
Visits to schools	1
Visits to ADS office	1

Table VI

DISTRICT SUPERINTENDENT QUESTIONNAIRE
DS RELATIONSHIPS AND INFORMAL MEETINGS
WITH TEACHERS
SAMPLE OF 8 DS, 1966

Relationships	*Number of DS*
Orientation teas	2
Rates probationary teachers	3
Approves principals' ratings of teachers	2
Visits teachers rated unsatisfactory	1
Visits teachers (without rating)	4
Evaluates programs	2
Organizes district workshops	4
Organizes in-service courses	2
Holds conferences and meetings	3
Has grievance procedures	2
Gives personal guidance	2
Places teachers on district committees	1
Contact with teachers through coordinators	1
Recommends teachers for advancement	1
Works with teachers on special projects	1

Informal Meetings[a]	
Orientation teas	6
Visits schools	4
When teachers are rated	2
Conferences	4
Staff meetings at ADS office	1
District committee meetings	1
Workshops	2
In-service courses	1

[a] *U.F.T. contract does not allow formal meetings between teachers and DS.*

Table VII
DISTRICT SUPERINTENDENT QUESTIONNAIRE
DS PERSONNEL DETERMINATION
CONCERNING TEACHERS[a]
SAMPLE OF 9 DS, 1966

Determination Made	Number of DS
Rated teachers	2
Recommended teachers for transfer	1
Dropped probationary teachers	1
None made	5

[a] *Teachers are assigned to schools by Board of Education. DS may transfer teachers within district with their approval.*

Table VIII

DISTRICT SUPERINTENDENT QUESTIONNAIRE
DS PERSONNEL DETERMINATION
CONCERNING PRINCIPALS[a]
SAMPLE OF 8 DS, 1966

Determination Made	Number of DS
Appointed principal	2
Rated principal	1
None made	5

[a] *DS appoints principal from a list of top 3 candidates.*

Table IX

DISTRICT SUPERINTENDENT QUESTIONNAIRE
DECISIONS CONCERNING OTHER PERSONNEL
SAMPLE OF 9 DS, 1966

Determination Made	Number of DS
Assigned librarians	1
Appointed Administrative Assistant	1
Appointed coordinators	2
Changed an OTP* position	1
Obtained special position for a project	1
Made special use of a person for a project	1
Requested guidance counselors	1
Requested personnel for additional classes and special services	4
None made	2

* *OTP. Other Teaching Position.*

88

Footnotes

CHAPTER I

1. Gabriel Almond and Sidney Verga, *The Civic Culture* (Boston: Little, Brown and Company, 1965), p. 3.

2. Nelson Polsby, *Community Power and Political Theory* (New Haven: Yale University Press, 1963); Thomas J. Anton, "Power, Pluralism and Local Politics," *Administrative Science Quarterly* (March 1963), pp. 425-457; Bert Swanson, ed., *Current Trends in Comparative Community Studies* (Kansas City: Community Studies Inc., 1962); Morris Janowitz, *Community Political Systems* (Glencoe: Free Press, 1961).

3. Edward Banfield, *Political Influence* (Glencoe: Free Press, 1961); Robert Dahl, *Who Governs?* (New Haven: Yale University Press, 1961); Wallace Sayre and Herbert Kaufman, *Governing New York City* (New York: Russell Sage Foundation, 1960).

4. Sayre and Kaufman, *ibid.,* p. 715.

5. David Easton, *A Systems Analysis of Political Life* (New York: John Wiley and Sons, Inc., 1965).

6. Robert Agger, "Political Research as Political Action," in Robert Cahill and Stephen P. Hencley, eds., *The Politics of Education in the Local Community* (Danville, Ill.: The Interstate Printers and Publishers, Inc., 1964), p. 215.

7. Although there is still a dearth of published studies on the politics of education, there are an increasing number of doctoral dissertations in educational administration on the subject. Published studies include: Stephen K. Bailey, Richard T. Frost, and Paul E. Marsh, *Schoolmen and Politics* (Syracuse: Syracuse University Press, 1961); Warner E. Mills, Jr. and Harry R. Davis, *Small City Government: Seven Cases in Decision-Making* (New York: Random House, 1962); Joseph Pois, *The School Board Crisis* (Chicago: Educational Methods Inc., 1964); Nicholas Masters, Robert H. Salisbury, and Thomas Eliot, *State Politics and The Public Schools* (New York: Alfred A. Knopf, 1964); Ralph B. Kimborough, "Development of a Concept of Social Power," in Cahill and Hencley, *op. cit.,* pp. 93-94; Keith Goldhammer, "Community Power Structure and School Board Membership," *American School Board Journal* (March 1955), pp. 23-25. For treatments concerned with the more general issue of community power and education see: Ronald F. Campbell, Luvern L. Cunningham, and Roderick F. McPhee, *The Organization and Control of American Schools* (Columbus: Charles E. Merrill Books, Inc., 1965); Cahill and Hencley, *op. cit.;* Ralph B. Kimborough, *Political Power and Educational Decision Making* (Chicago: Rand McNally and Co., 1964); Eugene R. Smoley, Jr., *Community Participation in Urban School Government* (Baltimore: John Hopkins University, 1965). For current research see the September, 1966, issue of *Urban Affairs Quarterly.*

8. Sayre and Kaufman, *op. cit.,* pp. 716-719.

CHAPTER II

1. Public expectations in this area were illustrated by an item in the *World Telegram and Sun* of May 29, 1963, reporting criticism by the Catholic Teachers Association of Mayor Wagner's failure to appoint a Catholic to replace a retiring member, Brendan Byrne. Months later, when a Jewish member of the Board retired, a Catholic was appointed thereby reestablishing the 3:3:3 balance.

2. The three Board presidents during the period from 1945 to 1961 later moved on to political office. Maximilian Moss was elected surrogate in Brooklyn, Arthur Levitt was elected state con-

troller, and Charles Silver became a personal advisor to the mayor. Such moves indicate not only the closeness of the men to the mayor but their active participation in the Democratic party.

3. For a discussion of this problem by a Chicago board member see Pois, *op. cit.*, pp. 42-56. Smoley *op. cit.*, pp. 170) notes that in Baltimore "the board does not consider many issues concerned with significant policy matters." In contrast to the position taken in this study, Swanson attributes an important role to the Board on the ground that they are subject to community complaints and pressures Bert Swanson, *School Integration Controversies in New York City* (Bronxville, N.Y.: Institute for Community Studies, Sarah Lawrence College), pp. 44-48.

4. *Education Law*, Section 2564, amended by L. 1961.

4a. The mass resignation of several local boards in New York low-income areas was accompanied by statements on the feeling of the board that they lacked power.

5. Sayre and Kaufman attribute the superintendent's limited powers to being circumscribed by the Board of Education, the Board of Superintendents (since abolished), and the teachers organizations. *Op. cit.*, p. 282.

6. Allen Talbott, "Needed: A New Breed of School Superintendents," *Harper's Magazine* (February 1966), pp. 81-87.

7. In interviews, Union leaders have indicated that they might be faced with vindictive action by the school superintendent if they conferred with Board members on school problems. This is not a problem confined to New York City. See Pois, *op. cit.*, pp. 118-123; Campbell, Cunningham, and McPhee, *op. cit.*, pp. 182-183; Neal Gross, *Who Runs Our Schools?* (New York: John Wiley and Sons, Inc., 1959); and Thomas R. Bowman, "Participation of Superintendents in School Board Decision Making," *Administrators' Notebook* (January 1963).

8. Talbott, *op. cit.*

9. Personal contact between Board members and the supervisory staff is far from uncommon. Several years ago the situation was so bad that the superintendent issued a statement halting memos that went directly from the staff to Board members. *World Telegram and Sun,* Nov. 15, 1963, p. 47.

10. *The New York Times,* October 20, 1966.

11. George Strayer and Louis Yavner, *Administrative Management of the School System of New York City* (1951) and *Modern Management for the City of New York,* Vol. II (1953); Office of the City Administrator, *Board of Education Organization and Management of School Planning and Construction* (1959); Education Commissioner's Committee on Inquiry into Charges of Waste and Extravagance in Construction of School Buildings in New York City, *School Construction in New York City* (1951); Mark Schinnerer, *A Report to the New York City Education Department* (1961).

12. In interviews, Board members indicated their concern with the enormous power of the supervisory staff and the system's inbred method of selection, but they despair of their ability to change the situation.

13. The present superintendent (Donovan) has taken several steps to enhance the position of the district superintendent by adding to the latter's staff and budgetary powers. Under new procedures the district superintendent is given the opportunity to distribute personnel and financial resources among the schools in his district as he sees fit. Whether or not the district superintendents will take advantage of these powers depends upon their willingness to take on responsibility for decision making. From responses to the questionnaire in this study, optimism is not warranted.

14. For an example of this influence: it was a lobbyist employed by the High School Chairmans Association who pushed through the "salary index" to become state policy. This index assures supervisors of a sliding scale for salaries, in relation to the rate of teachers' pay.

15. Both the High School Principals Association and the Junior High School Principals Association have expressed opposition to the 5-3-4 and 4-4-4 school reorganization plans. Several associations opposed the elimination of the I.Q. examination, school pairing proposals, and the comprehensive high school plan.

16. In interviews, most executive board members of the Union attributed little power to their organization except in salary matters. In most areas, they cited as wielders of power the Board of Education and the superintendent. See Alan Rosenthal, "Pedagogues and Power," *Urban Affairs Quarterly* (September 1966), for a study of Union officials' perceptions of the participants in school policymaking.

17. The United Parents Association has been most active in a campaign to prevent the use of federal and state aid for parochial schools *(The New York Times,* October 24, 1966). The Association is a recent recipient of a poverty grant to encourage parent participation in associations in economically disadvantaged communities. Development of this program may ultimately broaden the membership base of the Association and change its emphasis.

18. *Reorganizing Secondary Education in New York City* (Education Guidance and Work Committee of the Public Education Association, 1963).

19. *New York Herald Tribune,* June 8, 1965.

20. Pois, *op. cit.,* pp. 141-142.

CHAPTER III

1. Appendix A, Table II.

2. Appendix A, Table I.

3. State Education Commissioner's Advisory Committee on Human Relations and Community Tensions, *Desegregating the Public Schools of New York City* (May 1964), pp. 11 and 14.

4. Benjamin A. Bloom, Allison Davis, and Robert Hess, *Compensatory Education for Cultural Deprivation* (New York: Holt, Rinehart, and Winston, Inc., 1965), pp. 1-40.

5. Appendix A, Table I, and Eleanor Bernert Sheldon and Raymond A. Glazer, *Pupils and Schools in New York City. A Fact Book* (New York: Russell Sage Foundation, 1965), pp. 1-20. It should be noted that middle class Negroes also have been sending their children to private schools in increasing numbers. See Marilyn Gittell, "A Pilot Study of Negro Middle Class Attitudes Toward Higher Education," *Journal of Negro Education* (Fall 1965), pp. 385-94.

6. Appendix A, Tables V-XIV.

7. *The New York Times,* September 2, 1965. The Board released a report of its Research Bureau that showed the program had virtually no measurable effect on the achievement of pupils.

8. Nat Hentoff, "Profiles: The Principal," *The New Yorker* (May 7, 1966), pp. 52-119.

9. See footnote 11, chapter II, *supra,* for a complete listing.

10. *The New York Times,* October 21, 1965.

11. *New York Herald Tribune, op. cit.*

12. Other areas of policy were reviewed in a more cursory way to broaden the scope of the analysis. An area omitted which later proved to have been worthy of further exploration was school site selection and construction. This study reviewed such concerns only as it related to school integration and budgeting.

CHAPTER IV

1. Local Law No. 19 passed by the City Council on April 6, 1962, and reenacted each year since then, provided that the appropriation for the Board of Education in the mayor's proposed expense budget shall be a lump sum.

2. The 1963 memorandum also states that the mayor will not exercise any control on expenditures for the repair and maintenance of school facilities of less than $25,000 and the comptroller will not pre-audit any payment to be made by the Board for supplies or for the repair and maintenance of school facilities.

3. Aside from the requirement that the Board of Education organize its budget in accordance with instructions issued by the state Department of Education and the Board of Regents, which specifies broad program areas, there is no state control over the budget.

4. Special service schools are designated as such by a statistical index that includes measures of pupil mobility, per cent of pupils receiving free lunches, the number of teachers on permanent license, the per cent of non-English speaking pupils, and results from I.Q. and reading tests. Sheldon and Glazier, *op. cit.*, p. 32.

5. The individuals are the assistant superintendents for: curriculum, special education, primary education, intermediate education, and senior high schools.

6. The information for this analysis was accumulated in interviews and visits to the Office of Business Affairs.

7. Generally, the Board views its role as one of assuring that there will be city financial support for the total budget, thereby satisfying staff requests and such public pressures as there are. Not to be underestimated in the development of high school curriculum is the state regents' policy. Much of what is taught in New York City high schools is determined by the content of the regents' examination.

8. H. Thomas Jones, James A. Kelly, and Walter Garms, *Determinants of Educational Expenditures in Large Cities in the United States* (Stanford: School of Education, Stanford University, 1966).

9. George A. Beauchamp, *Planning the Elementary School Curriculum.* (New York: Allyn and Bacon, 1956), p. 10.

10. *Ibid.*

11. See Carl Marburger, "Considerations for Educational Planning," in August Kerber and Barbara Bommarito, eds., *The Schools and the Urban Crisis* (New York: Holt, Rinehart, and Winston, 1965), pp. 259-260. Marburger emphasizes the need for involvement of the total staff to achieve innovation in curriculum. He also points to the importance of community involvement.

CHAPTER V

1. Theodore Lowi, *At the Pleasure of the Mayor* (New York: The Free Press of Glencoe, 1964).

2. His father had been an assistant superintendent in the system, and he himself was a close associate of the mayor.

3. *New York Herald Tribune,* October 1, 1957; *New York Sun,* December 16, 1946.

4. *New York Herald Tribune,* January 15, 1947.

5. Much of the information used in this description was taken from the files of the Public Education Association and from the *New York Telegram and Sun,* December 12, 1956, and December 27, 1956; and *The New York Times,* September 13, 1957, and September 20, 1957.

6. There was a grass roots teachers' movement under the teachers union in 1949-50, that at that time achieved a $995 increase in salaries. In 1953 the superintendent refused to negotiate with the various groups separately, and a merger agreement was arranged that provided the basis for representation by a single organization.

7. See footnote 14, chapter II, *supra.*

CHAPTER VI

1. The recommendations were:

a) To raise the level of academic achievement in the Negro and Puerto Rican schools through an intensive educational program developed by the superintendent of schools and his staff;

b) To reexamine the procedures by which children were placed in adjustment and opportunity classes and in the intellectually gifted and Special Progress classes (children in the CRMD classes to be reexamined within a year);

c) That the Board should establish for each grade definite limits within which certain modifications were permitted and certain requirements made mandatory;

d) To formulate a new minimum guidance program for schools with enrollments largely from underprivileged groups;

e) To encourage children of all faiths and ethnic origins to prepare for positions as teachers and guidance counsellors;

f) To provide more extensive and intensive programs of mental testing, observation, and other such techniques;

g) That the Board of Education should continue studies to measure the incidence of successful college candidates coming from high schools of different ethnic groups and different socioeconomic backgrounds;

h) That the commission and the Board should sponsor a demonstration project in the early identification and intensified continued guidance of able students in as many junior high schools as possible;

i) To select new school sites so as to facilitate enrollment by mixed ethnic groups;

j) To give high priority to the modernization of older schools and the construction of new ones in areas of mixed ethnic population-modernization to include a maximum provision for special classrooms, kindergartens, lunchrooms, play areas, and sanitary facilities;

k) That the agencies involved in planning for physical plant take into consideration projected population changes;

l) That the Board of Education should request appropriations for adequate school maintenance as well as for new plant construction;

m) To provide "subject" schools with additional supervisory, nonteaching, and other positions;

n) To provide a parking area in the vicinity of every school within a congested area of the city for the use of school personnel;

o) That applicants for promotion to supervisory positions should be required to serve a three-year period in the subject schools;

p) That a ratio of regular to substitute teachers be established for each division and that an adequate number of permanent licensees be assigned to each school;

q) That appointments should be based solely on measured ability regardless of race or creed, and as far as possible that the staffing of schools should reflect the heterogeneous nature of the city's population;

r) That the Board should issue a policy statement pointing out that a positive attitude toward all groups, regardless of race, religion, or national origin, is a prerequisite for appointment or promotion to supervisory positions;

s) That teacher training institutions should be alerted to the need that their students possess informed attitudes in the field of race relations;

t) That the Board should establish courses in human relations and intercultural understanding for all persons beginning service in the city's school system;

u) That the Division of Personnel should institute a specific permanent recruitment unit;

v) That in addition to the traditional objectives of zoning, the Board should establish as a cardinal principle the objective of integration;

w) That a comprehensive zoning plan, to be formulated by the superintendent of schools, should be administered by a new professional bureau, the Central Zoning Unit;

x) That an Advisory Council on Zoning, organized on a city-wide basis, should be established;

y) That an expanded centralized community relations unit be created to help assistant superintendents and principals in developing community relations programs;

z) That a Public Information Unit be organized within the Board to disseminate through the press, radio, television, and other media information relating to its policy determinations and to the administration of the school system.

Board of Education of the City of New York, *Toward the Integration of Our Schools; Final Report of the Commission on Integration* (June 1965).

2. Views expressed at the Board hearings pointed to the sources of support and opposition that were to follow. Most notable in this respect was the strong civic-group support for the proposal by the United Parents Association, the Public Education Association, the Citizens Committee for Children, the Intergroup Committee on New York Public Schools, and the American Jewish Congress. Spokesmen for the leading teachers groups attacked the plans. *The New York Times*, January 18, 1957.

3. *The New York Times*, April 23, 1957; May 5, 1958; and January 30, 1959.

4. See daily reports in *The New York Times* during this period.

5. *The New York Times*, March 3, 1964.

6. In 1958 Justice Polier decided in favor of the parents action, citing deficiencies in ghetto schools as adequate justification for withdrawing their children. *The New York Times*, December 15, 1958.

7. *Ibid.*, September 1 and 2, 1960.

8. In September 1964, with a revised and enlarged program, 110,000 pupils were offered the opportunity to transfer; 2,000 applied and 1,800 were transferred. State Commissions Advisory Committee on Human Relations and Community Tensions, *op. cit.*

9. The United Parents Association stated its policy position in a booklet issued in the middle of 1961, calling for transfer of Negro children to schools in white neighborhoods.

10. Board members who were questioned in the course of this study noted the practical problems obstructing the implementation of their integration policy. They also pointed to staff inaction as a cause for delay. A member of the Board stated that were she not on the Board she would probably be out on the picket line, but dealing with the tough problem of ironing out procedures had taken the edge off her dedication to implementation.

11. New York City Public Schools, *Blueprint for Further Action Toward Quality Integrated Education —* Recommendations of the superintendent of schools to the Board of Education (1965).

12. David Rogers, a study on school integration in New York City, forthcoming from the Center for Urban Education. See also Sheldon, *et al.*, "Administrative Implications of Integration Plans for Schools," in Albert J. Reiss, Jr., ed., *Schools in a Changing Society* (New York: The Free Press of Glencoe, 1965).

13. State Commissioner's Committee on Human Relations and Community Tensions, *op. cit.,* p. 5.

14. *Ibid.*

15. Bernard E. Donovan, *Implementation of Board Policy on Excellence for the City's Schools* — Report to the Board of Education (April 28, 1965).

CHAPTER VII

1. Lowi, *op. cit.,* p. 200. Lowi suggests that reform mayors and federal or state action are the major forces for change in New York City.

2. This study did not evaluate the potential significance of federal policy. Under Titles I and III of the Elementary and Secondary Education Act of 1965, federal aid arrangements require that programs be developed in cooperation with local community groups. Although funds are appropriated to the Board of Education, the guidelines strongly state the intention of establishing continuous and genuine working relations between school officials and community groups. The anti-poverty program has also encouraged the opening of channels of communication between the schools, schoolmen, and other local groups. The full consequences of these efforts are not yet apparent, but the general approach appears to offer extremely significant avenues for broadening the scope and character of school policy. In October 1965, however, the anti-poverty operations board in New York City criticized the Board of Education because it had not consulted with them in regard to the Board's federally financed programs.

3. Masters, Salisbury, and Eliot, *op. cit.* Their study reviews the role of state educational officers in local school policy in Michigan, Illinois, and Missouri. James Conant's concern with the monopoly of the professional educators is particularly relevant. The professionals run the local school systems, control government policy in state administrative posts, and direct the teachers colleges.

4. State Education Commissioner's Advisory Committee on Human Rights and Community Tensions, *op. cit.*

5. In a recent controversy in a Harlem school, the Mayor was criticized by the Board for interfering with the situation, and the Board noted in defense of its authority that it was a state agency. However, when the state commissioner issued a statement critical of Board action, it ignored his recommendations. *The New York Times,* September 23, 24, 27, 28, 30, 1966.

6. Michael D. Usdan, *The Political Power of Education in New York State* (New York: Institute of Administrative Research, Teachers College, Columbia University, 1963).

7. Strayer and Yavner, *Administrative Management of the School System of New York City,* Vol. I (New York: Mayor's Management Survey Commission, 1951).

8. *Local Law No. 19.* Passed by the City Council on April 6, 1962.

9. *Education Law,* Section 2553, subdivision 1, 2, amended L. 1961.

10. A scanning of three years of school news stories in two New York City papers reveals that the Mayor's public statements were almost always in response to public pressures. Some observers have suggested that the Mayor's noninvolvement was selective and based on a measuring of political advantage. This would not contradict the conclusion here, since in most cases there would be little direct political advantage to a mayor were he to become involved. There are also those who suggest that positive and constructive school policies were never forthcoming from the Mayor though he continued to be involved in an informal way on minor issues. This position is not controverted by the conclusions drawn in this study.

11. *The New York Times,* March 1, 1965.

12. Banfield, *op. cit.* There is some suggestion that the mayor functions as a mediator because he recognizes this is all his powers will allow him to do.

13. Several school politicians have suggested that the new procedure for selection of Board members has effectively undermined the role of the Catholic church in school policy.

14. This was clearly demonstrated in the recent activities of Project Headstart in New York City. Although the Board of Education is responsible for more than half the Headstart children and facilities, interested civic groups virtually ignored Board policies, concentrating their attention and efforts on the private-agency Headstart centers.

CHAPTER VIII

1. Sayre and Kaufman, *op. cit.,* p. 285.

2. Agger, Goldrich, and Swanson, *op. cit.,* p. 73.

3. Sayre and Kaufman, *op. cit.,* p. 720.

4. See Harry Scoble, "Some Questions for Researchers," in Cahill and Hencley, eds., *op. cit.,* pp. 111-124; David Minar, "Community Characteristics, Conflict, and Power Structure," *ibid.,* pp. 125-143; and David Rogers, "Community Political Systems: A Framework and Hypothesis for Comparative Studies," in Bert Swanson, ed., *op. cit.,* pp. 31-48.

5. Norton Long, "The Local Community as an Ecology of Games," *American Journal of Sociology* (November 1957), pp. 251-261.

6. Minar, *op. cit.*

7. *Ibid.,* p. 133.

8. Norton Long, *Public Administration Review* (Winter 1961), pp. 23-30.

9. T. E. Hollander, "Fiscal Independence in Large City School Systems," in Marilyn Gittell, ed., *Educating an Urban Society* (Beverly Hills: Sage Publications, 1967); H. Thomas James, J. Alan Thomas, and Harold J. Dyck, *Wealth, Expenditure and Decision Making for Education* (Stanford, California: School of Education, Stanford University, 1963).

9a. In his Baltimore study, Smoley (*op. cit.,* pp. 48-56) found little direct participation in school board decisions and no participation on the part of business notables.

10. Minar, *op. cit.,* p. 131. See also Robert H. Salisbury, "Urban Politics and Education," in Sam Bass Warner, Jr., ed., *Planning for a Nation of Cities* (Cambridge, Mass.: Massachusetts Institute of Technology Press, 1966), pp. 268-284.

11. Peter Schrag, "Boston, Education's Last Hurrah," *Saturday Review* (May 21, 1966), pp. 56-58, 74-76; Robert Havinghurst, *The Public Schools of Chicago* (Chicago: Board of Education, 1964).

12. Robert Dahl, *op. cit.,* pp. 155-159; Sayre and Kaufman, *op. cit.,* p. 284; Pois, *op. cit.,* pp. 124-145.

13. Joseph Marr Cronin, *The Board of Education in the Great Cities,* Unpublished E.ED. dissertation (Stanford University, June 1965); Keith Goldhammer, *The School Board* (New York: The Center for Applied Research in Education, Inc., 1964).

14. Pois, *op. cit.*

15. *Baltimore Sun,* January 2, 1960.

16. Pois, *op. cit.,* p. 125.

17. Gross, *op. cit.,* p. 159.

18. Thomas R. Bowman, *op. cit.*

19. Talbott, *op. cit.*

20. Cronin, *op. cit.,* pp. 280-294.

21. Banfield, *op. cit.,* maintains that the party serves as the centralizing force in Chicago politics, but it seems not to play that role any longer in school policy.

Bibliography

I. POLITICS

Agger, Robert E., Daniel Goldrich, and Bert E. Swanson. *The Rulers and the Ruled; Political Power and Impotence in American Communities.* New York: John Wiley and Sons, 1964.

Anton, Thomas J. "Power, Pluralism, and Local Politics," *Administrative Science Quarterly,* VII (March, 1963), pp. 425-457.

Bailey, Stephen K., Richard T. Frost, Paul E. Marsh, and Robert C. Wood. *Schoolmen and Politics; A Study of State Aid to Education in the Northeast.* Syracuse: Syracuse University Press, 1962.

Banfield, Edward C. *Big City Politics.* New York: Random House, 1965.

Banfield, Edward C. *Political Influence.* Glencoe: Free Press, 1961.

Belknap, George and Ralph Smuckler. "Political Power Relations in a Mid-Western City," *Public Opinion Quarterly,* XX (Spring, 1956), pp. 73-81.

Brown, Gilbert Clark. *Decision-Making by the Board of Education and Administration of the Springvale, New York Public Schools.* Doctoral Dissertation, Teachers College, Columbia University, New York: 1959-60.

Cahill, Robert S. and Stephen P. Hencley, editors. *The Politics of Education in the Local Community.* Danville: Interstate Printers and Publishers, 1964.

Campbell, R. F. *Government of Public Education for Adequate Policy Making* ("Processes of Policy Making Within Structures of Educational Government"). Urbana, Illinois: Bureau of Educational Research, University of Illinois, 1960.

Campbell, R.F. "Methods Used to Nominate and Elect Local School Boards," *American School Board Journal,* CXX (March, 1950), pp. 27-28.

Campbell, R.F. and John Ramseyer. *The Dynamics of School Community Relationships.* New York: Allyn and Bacon, 1955.

Chaput, D.C. "Who Determines Policy?" *Clearing House,* XXXVII (May, 1963), pp. 521-522.

Cicourel, Aaron V. and John I. Kitsuse. *The Educational Decision-Makers.* Indianapolis: The Bobbs-Merrill Company, 1963.

Cleary, R.E. "Conflicting Pressures: the Educator and Politics," *Peabody's Journal of Education,* XL (May, 1963), pp. 323-329.

Curle, A. "Education, Politics, and Development," *Comparative Education Review,* VII (February, 1964), pp. 226-245.

Dahl, Robert. *Who Governs? Democracy and Power in an American City.* New Haven: Yale University Press, 1961.

Easton, David. *A Systems Analysis of Political Life.* New York: John Wiley and Sons, 1965.

Educational Policies Commission. *Citizens and Educational Policies.* Washington, D.C.: NEA and AASA, 1951.

Eliot, Thomas H. "Towards an Understanding of Public School Politics," *Teachers College Record,* LXII (November, 1960), pp. 118-132.

Exton, E. "Are Local School Boards on the Way Out?" *American School Board Journal,* CXXXXLVII (April, 1964), pp. 19-20.

Fillerup, Joseph McDonald *Community Groups and their Relationship to School Quality.* Typewritten Report. New York: Teachers College, Columbia University, 1956.

Forces Affecting American Education. Washington, D.C.: Association for Supervision and Curriculum Development, 1953 Yearbook.

Gleaser, Jr., E. J. *The Identification of Certain Alignments of Social Power Impinging Upon Decision-Making of School Committee and Superintendent in a New England Community.* Doctoral Dissertation. Harvard University, 1953.

Goldhammer, K. "Community Power Structure and School Board Membership," *American School Board Journal,* CXXX (March, 1955), pp. 23-25.

Gross, N.C. *Who Runs Our Schools?* New York: Wiley; London: Chapman, 1958.

Haussler, Kenneth S. "Local Control of Public Schools," *The American School Board Journal,* CXLVII (October, 1963), pp. 9-12.

Henry, Nelson B., editor. *Social Forces Influencing American Education.* 60th Yearbook of the National Society for the Study of Education. Chicago: University of Chicago Press, 1961.

Hodgkinson, Harold L. *Educational Decisions: A Casebook.* Englewood Cliffs: Prentice Hall, 1963.

Hunter, Floyd. *Community Power Structure: A Study of Decision-Makers.* Chapel Hill: University of North Carolina Press, 1953.

Janowitz, Morris. *Community Political Systems.* Glencoe: Free Press, 1961.

Kammerer, Gladys M., Charles Farris, John Degrove, and Alfred Clubok. *The Urban Political Community; Profiles in Town Politics.* Boston: Houghton Miflin Company, 1963.

Kimbrough, Ralph B. *Political Power and Educational Decision-Making.* Chicago: Rand McNally and Company, 1964.

Lindquist, Donald Mark. *Development of an Instrument to Measure Group Participation in Administrative Decision-Making in Public Schools.* Doctoral Dissertation, Teachers College, Columbia University, New York: 1960-61.

Lowi, Theodore. *At the Pleasure of the Mayor: Patronage and Power in New York City, 1898-1958.* New York: The Free Press of Glencoe, 1964.

MacKinnon, F. *The Politics of Education, A Study of the Political Administration of Public Schools.* Toronto: University of Toronto Press, 1960.

Martin, Roscoe, Frank Munger, and others. *Decisions in Syracuse.* Bloomington: Indiana University Press, 1961.

Martin, Roscoe. *Government and the Suburban School.* Syracuse: Syracuse University Press, 1962.

Masters, Nicholas A., Robert H. Salisbury, and Thomas H. Eliot. *State Politics and the Public Schools, an Exploratory Analysis.* New York: A. Knopf, 1964.

Miller, Alfred. *Patterns in Budget-Making: A Study of Public Involvement.* Doctoral Dissertation, Teachers College, Columbia University, New York: 1957-58.

Miller, Delbert C. "Decision-Making Cliques in Community Power Structures A Comparative Study of an American and English City," *American Journal of Sociology,* LXIV (November, 1958), pp. 299-310.

Milb, Jr., Warner E. and Harry R. Davis, *Small City Government: Seven Cases in Decision-Making.* New York: Random House, 1962.

Patrick, T.L. "When Is an Independent School Board Independent?" *American School Board Journal,* CXXXII (April, 1956), pp. 27-29.

Polsby, Nelson. *Community Power and Political Theory.* New Haven: Yale University Press, 1963.

Presthus, Robert. *Men at the Top: A Study in Community Power.* New York: Oxford University Press, 1964.

Remmlein, M.K. "Can the Government Legally Control Education," *School Executive,* LXXIX (October, 1959), pp. 64-65.

Roach, Stephen F. "Conflicts Between School Districts and Municipalities," *The American School Board Journal,* CXXXIX (July, 1959), p. 33.

Rosenthal, Alan. "Pedagogues and Power," *Urban Affairs Quarterly,* II (September, 1966).

Rosenthal, Alan. *Unpublished Manuscript on the Role of Teachers' Organizations in School Policy-Making.* Hunter College, New York.

Rossi, Peter H. "Community Decision-Making," *Administrative Science Quarterly,* I (March, 1957), pp. 415-443.

Sayre, Wallace S. "Politics of Education," *Teachers College Record,* LXV (November, 1963), pp. 178-183.

Sayre, Wallace S. and Herbert Kaufman. *Governing New York City: Politics in the Metropolis.* New York: Russell Sage Foundation, 1960.

Smith, Max S. and William R. Smittle. *The Board of Education and Educational Policy Development.* Ann Arbor: Edwards Brothers, 1954.

Spalding, W.B. *Improving Public Education Through School Board Action* "The School Board as Policy-Making Body." Pittsburgh: University of Pittsburgh Press, 1950.

Usdan, Michael D. *The Political Power of Education In New York State.* New York: The Institute of Administrative Research, Teachers College, Columbia University, 1963.

Walton, J. *Administration and Policy-Making in Education.* Baltimore: Johns Hopkins Press, 1959.

Warner, William Lloyd and others. *Democracy in Jonesville.* New York: Harper and Brothers, 1949.

White, Alpheus L. *Local School Boards: Organization and Practices.* Washington, D.C.: United States Office of Education, 1962.

Willbern, York. "Education and the American Political System," *Teachers College Record,* LIX (February, 1958), pp. 292-298.

II. ADMINISTRATION

Administrative Practices in Urban School Districts. Washington, D.C.: National Education Association, 1961.

Allen, Jr., James E. "The School Board in Today's World," *School and Society,* XC (February 10, 1962), pp. 48-50.

Austin, David B. *American High School Administration.* New York: Holt, Rinehart, and Winston, 1961.

Bruce, William C. Editorial, "School Administration Decisions," *The American School Board Journal,* CXLI (November, 1960), p. 40.

Burr, J.B. *Elementary School Administration.* Boston: Allyn and Bacon, 1963.

Callahan, R.E. *Education and the Cult of Efficiency: A Study of the Social Forces That Have Shaped the Administration of Public Schools.* Chicago: University of Chicago Press, 1962.

Campbell, R.F. and R.T. Gregg. *Administrative Behavior in Education.* New York: Harper and Brothers, 1957.

Campbell, R.F. "Educational Administration: Is It Unique?" *School Review,* LXVII (Winter, 1959), pp. 461-468.

Campbell, R.F., John Corbally, Jr., and John Ramseyer, *Introduction to Educational Administration.* Boston: Allyn and Bacon, 1962.

Campbell, R.F., Luvern L. Cunningham, and R.F. McPhee. *The Organization and Control of American Schools.* Columbus: Charles E. Merrill, 1965.

Castether, William B. *Administering the School Personnel Program.* New York: MacMillan, 1962.

Cooperative Program in Educational Administration: Middle Atlantic Region. Teachers College, Columbia University, New York: 1954.

Counts, George S. *Decision-Making and American Values in School Administration.* New York: Published for the Cooperative Program in Educational Administration, Middle Atlantic Region by the Bureau of Publications, Teachers College, Columbia University, 1954.

Culbertson, Jack A., Paul B. Jacobson, and Theodore Reller. *Administrative Relationships: A Casebook.* Englewood Cliffs: Prentice Hall (Educational Series), 1960.

Dykes, Archie. "Of School Boards and Superintendents," *Teachers College Record,* LXVI (February, 1965), pp. 399-400.

"Educational Administration as Public Administration," book review from Austin, David B., Will French, and J. Dan Hull, *American High School Administration,* Third Edition, in *School and Society,* LXXXIX (December 16, 1961), pp. 438-440.

Grieder, C. and others. *Public School Administration.* New York: Ronald Press, 1954.

Halpin, A.W., editor. *Administrative Theory in Education.* Chicago: Midwest Administration Center, University of Chicago, 1958.

Jackson, James B. *A Study of Administrative Organization in Nine Selected Public School Systems.* Typewritten Report. New York: Teachers College, Columbia University, 1956.

Jensen, Gale. "Dangers of Too Much Administration," *University of Michigan School of Education Bulletin,* (October, 1961), pp. 3-6.

Kerr, Norman. "The School Board as an Agency of Legitimation," *Sociology of Education,* XXXVIII (Fall, 1964), pp. 34-59.

Lindenfeld, Frank. "Does Administrative Staff Grow as Fast as Organization?" *School Life,* XLIII (May, 1961), pp. 20-23.

McClennan, George Bruce. *The Relation of Factors in the Organizational Pattern of School Systems and Adaptability.* Doctoral Dissertation, Teachers College, Columbia University, New York: 1952.

Miller, W. I. *Democracy in Educational Administration: An Analysis of Principles and Practices.* New York: Bureau of Publications, Teachers College, Columbia University, 1942.

Moore, Jr., H. A. *Studies in School Administration.* Washington, D. C.: American Association of School Administrators, 1957.

Morely, F. P. and others. "Roles of Supervisors and Administrators," *Association of Supervisors and Curriculum Development Yearbook,* (1964), pp. 125-158.

Newlon, J. H. *Educational Administration as Social Policy.* New York: Charles Scribners Sons, 1934.

Ovsiew, L. *Emerging Practices in School Administration.* New York: Metropolitan School Study Council and Cooperative Program in Educational Administration, 1953.

Ramseyer, John and others. *Factors Affecting Educational Administration and Guide Posts to Research and Action.* (The Cooperative Program in Educational Administration, School Community Development monograph #2.) Columbus: College of Education, Ohio State University, 1955.

Reeder, W. G. *The Fundamentals of Public School Administration.* (Fourth Edition) New York: Macmillan, 1958.

Reller, T. L. *Comparative Educational Administration.* Englewood Cliffs: Prentice Hall, 1962.

Ross, Donald H., editor. *Administration for Adaptability.* New York: Metropolitan School Study Council, 1958.

Sargent, Cyril G. and E. L. Belisle. *Educational Administration: Cases and Concepts.* Boston: Houghton Mifflin Company, 1955.

Saunders, J., editor. "How Can We Streamline Administration in New York City Schools?" *New York Society for the Experimental Study of Education Yearbook,* (1961), pp. 1-4.

Sayre, Wallace S. "Additional Observations on the Study of Administration," *Teachers College Record,* LX (November, 1958), pp. 73-76.

Sears, J. B. "The Nature of the Administrative Process in Education: A Partial Analysis of the Factors Involved," *Educational Administration and Supervision,* XXXI (January, 1945), pp. 1-21.

Shafer, Hugh M. "The Role of Administration in Policy Making," *The American School Board Journal,* CXXXIX (November, 1959), pp. 19-20.

Sheldon, Eleanor Bernert and others. "Administrative Implications of Integration Plans for Schools," *Schools in a Changing Society.* Albert J. Reiss, Jr., editor, New York: The Free Press of Glencoe, 1965.

Smith, G. A. *Policy Formation and Administration.* Chicago: Richard and Irwin, 1951.

Spaulding, F. *School Superintendent in Action in Five Cities.* New York: Richard B. Smith, 1955.

Miller, Van and W. B. Spalding. *The Public Administration of American Schools.* (Second Edition), Yonkers-on-the-Hudson: World Book Company, 1958.

Wahlquist, John T. *The Administration of Public Education.* New York: Ronald Press, 1952.

Walton, J. "The Theoretical Study of Educational Administration," *Harvard Education Review,* XXV (Summer, 1955), pp. 169-178.

White, Alpheus L. *Local School Boards: Organization and Practices.* Washington, D. C.: United States Government Printing Office, 1962.

Wilson, L. C. *Community Power Controls Related to the Administration of Education.* Doctoral Dissertation, George Peabody College for Teachers, Nashville: 1952.

Wynn, R. *Organization of Public Schools.* Washington, D. C.: Center for Applied Research in Education, 1964.

Your Schools and Staffing: Current Practice in Administrative Staffing in New York State. Albany: CDPSA, 1955.

III. GENERAL

Aho, F. *A Study of Community Forces in a School District During a Period of District Reorganization.* Unpublished Masters Thesis, Ohio State University, Columbus: 1954.

Almond, Gabriel and Sidney Verba. *The Civic Culture.* Boston: Little, Brown and Company, 1965.

Anderson, Vivienne. *Patterns of Educational Leadership.* Englewood Cliffs: Prentice Hall, 1956.

Ayer, F. L. *An Analysis of Controllable Community Factors Related to Quality of Education.* Doctoral Dissertation, Teachers College, Columbia University, New York: 1950.

Baltimore Sun. January 2, 1960.

Beach, F. F. *The State and Education.* Washington, D.C.: United States Department of Health, Education and Welfare, 1955.

Beauchamp, George A. *Planning the Elementary School Curriculum.* New York: Allyn and Bacon, 1956.

Beck, H. P. *School Boards.* New York: Kings Crown Press, 1947.

Blackwood, Paul E. "Conference of Large City Elementary School Supervisors," *School Life,* XLIII (June, 1961), pp. 12-15.

Bloom, Benjamin, Allison Davis, and Robert Hess. *Compensatory Education for Cultural Deprivation.* New York: Holt, Rinehart, and Winston, 1965.

Bloomberg, Warner and others. *Suburban Power Structure and Public Education* (Monograph series on Economics and Politics). Syracuse: Syracuse University Press, 1963.

Bruce, William C. Editorial, "Better City School Support," *The American School Board Journal,* CXLVII (October, 1963), p. 43.

Bruce, William C. Editorial, "City Superintendents in Large Cities," *The American School Board Journal,* CXLIII (August, 1961), p. 37.

Campbell, R. F. "Methods Used to Nominate and Elect Local School Board Members," *American School Board Journal,* CXX (March, 1950), p.28.

Campbell, R. F. *The Social Implications of School Board Legislation.* Doctoral Dissertation, Stanford University, Palo Alto: 1942.

Campbell, R. F. "The Superintendent — His Role and Professional Status," *Teachers College Record,* LXV (May, 1964), pp. 671-679.

Chandler, B. J., L. J. Stiles, and J. I. Kitsuse. *Education in Urban Society.* New York: Dodd, Mead and Company, 1962.

Changing Demands on Education and Their Fiscal Implications. A report prepared by John F. Norton for the National Committee for Support of the Public Schools. Washington, D.C.: 1963.

Charters, Jr., W. W. "Social Class Analysis and the Control of Public Education," *Harvard Education Review,* XXIII (Fall, 1953), pp. 268-283.

Cocking, W. *Regional Introduction of Educational Practices in Urban School Systems of the United States.* New York: Institute of Administrative Research, Study #6, Bureau of Publications, Teachers College, Columbia University, 1951.

Conant, James B. *Slums and Suburbs: A Commentary on Schools in Metropolitan Areas*. New York: McGraw Hill, 1961.

Cronin, Joseph Marr. *The Board of Education in the Great Cities*. Doctoral Dissertation, Stanford University, Palo Alto: June, 1965.

Davies, D. R. *Practical School Board Procedures*. New York: Chartwell House, 1951.

Davis, B. F. *Community Forces in a Recently Organized School District*. Masters Thesis, Ohio State University, Columbus: 1954.

Dewar, John A. "When Teachers Help Plan the Curriculum," *Educational Leadership*, XIX (October, 1961), pp. 5-7.

Donaldson, M. G. "Educators and School Board Elections," *Michigan Education Journal*, XLI (May, 1964), pp. 34-35.

Ferrer, Terry. "Calvin Gross — New Boss of the World's Largest School System," *Saturday Review*, XLV (December 15, 1962), pp. 47-49.

Financing Public Education in New York State. Albany: Temporary Commission on Educational Finances, 1956.

Gittell, Marilyn. *Educating an Urban Population*. Beverly Hills: Sage Publications, 1966.

Gittell, Marilyn. "A Pilot Study of Negro Middle Class Attitudes Toward Higher Education in New York," *The Journal of Negro Education*, XXXIV (Fall, 1965), pp. 385-394.

Goldhammer, Keith. *The School Board*. New York: The Center for Applied Research in Education, 1964.

Harris, W. D. "Urban Growth and City School Design," *American School and University Annual*, XXXIV (1962), pp. 37-42.

Havighurst, Robert J. *The Public Schools of Chicago*. Chicago: The Board of Education of the City of Chicago, 1964.

Henry, Nelson B., editor. *Social Forces Influencing American Education*. 60th Yearbook of the National Society for the Study of Education. Chicago: University of Chicago Press, 1961.

Hentoff, Nat. "Profiles: The Principal," *New Yorker Magazine* (May 7, 1966), pp. 52-119.

Hull, J. H. "Educational Leadership and Modern Society," *School and Society,* XC (September 22, 1962), pp. 292-293.

James, H. Thomas, J. Allan Thomas, and Harold J. Dyck. *Wealth, Expenditure and Decision Making for Education.* Stanford: School of Education, Stanford University, 1963.

James, H. Thomas, James A. Kelly, and Walter Garms. *Determinants of Educational Expenditures in Large Cities in the United States.* Stanford: School of Education, Stanford University, 1966.

Jones, David B. "Curriculum Innovations in a Public School System; Theory Into Practice," *Education Digest,* I (October, 1962), pp. 197-201.

Kalich, Perry M. *Teacher Assignment in Large Public School Systems.* New York: Report for Teachers College, Columbia University, 1962.

Kerber, August and Barbara Bommarito. *The Schools and the Urban Crisis.* New York: Holt, Rinehart, and Winston, 1965.

Kreitlow, W. B. "Reorganization Makes a Difference; Summary of Study by University of Wisconsin," *National Education Association Journal,* L (March, 1961), p. 55.

Landerholm, Merle Edwin. *A Study of Selected Elementary Secondary and School District Professional Staff Deployment Patterns.* New York: Teachers College, Columbia University, 1960.

Leomer, James A. *The Development of an Instrument to Secure Information on Certain Characteristics of Superintendents of Schools Which Relate to Program Improvement Activities.* Doctoral Dissertation, Teachers College, Columbia University, New York: 1956-57.

Lynd, Robert S. and Helen M. Lynd. *Middletown in Transition: A Study in Cultural Conflicts.* New York: Harcourt Brace, 1937.

Manual for the Study of Educational Dynamics of Communities. New York: Metropolitan School Study Council, Teachers College, Columbia University, 1944.

Massick, J. D. *The Discretionary Power of School Boards.* Durham: Duke University Press, 1949.

Mort, Paul R. *Educational Adaptability.* New York: Metropolitan School Study Council, 1953.

Mort, Paul R. *Fiscal Readiness for the Stress of Change.* Pittsburgh: University of Pittsburgh Press, 1957.

Newlon, Richard and Betty Jean Lee. "Denver Achieves Professional Negotiations," *National Education Association Journal,* LII (February, 1963), pp. 14-16.

Pierce, T. M. *Community Leadership for Public Education.* Englewood Cliffs: Prentice Hall, 1955.

Pierce, T. M. *Controllable Community Characteristics Related to the Quality of Education.* Metropolitan School Study Council Research Study No. 1. New York: Bureau of Publications, Teachers College, Columbia University, 1947.

Pois, Joseph. *The School Board Crisis: A Chicago Case Study.* Chicago: Educational Methods, 1964.

Public Administration Review. Winter 1961.

Reeder, W. G. *School Boards and Superintendents.* New York: Macmillan, 1954.

Reeves, C. E. *School Boards: Their Status, Functions and Activities.* Englewood Cliffs: Prentice Hall, 1954.

Schrag, Peter. "Boston: Education's Last Hurrah," *Saturday Review,* XLIX (May 21, 1966), pp. 56-58.

Shannon, J. R. "What 1,000 Terre Haute Citizens Look for in Voting for School Board Members," *American School Board Journal,* CXIV (February, 1947), pp. 29-30.

Shannon, W. A. "Education as School Boards See It," *School Executive,* LXXVIII (June, 1959), pp. 62-63.

Smoley, Jr., Eugene R. *Community Participation in Urban School Government.* Baltimore: John Hopkins University, 1965.

Spalding, Howard G. "Role of the Principal in Curriculum Week," *Teachers College Record,* LVIII (December, 1956), pp. 153-158.

Stapley, M. E. *School Board Studies.* Chicago: Midwest Administration Center, University of Chicago, 1957.

Swanson, Bert, editor. *Current Trends in Comparative Community Studies.* Kansas City: Community Studies, Inc., 1962.

Talbott, Allan R. "Needed: A New Breed of School Superintendent," *Harper's Magazine*, CCXXXII (February, 1966), pp. 81-87.

Walder, David LeRoy. *A Study of Professional Staff Development in the Associated Public School Systems*. New York: Report for Teachers College, Columbia University, 1961.

Westby, Cleve O. *Local Autonomy for School Communities in Cities: An Inquiry into Educational Potentials, Channels of Communication and Leeway for Local Action*. New York: Metropolitan School Study Council, Teachers College, Columbia University, 1947.

White, A. L. "An Analysis of School Board Organization: Trends and Developments in School Boards Organizations and Practices in Cities with a Population of 100,000 or More," *American School Board Journal*, CXLVI (April, 1963), pp. 7-8.

Wilson, C. H. "The Superintendent's Many Publics," *Saturday Review*, XLIV (October 21, 1961), pp. 49-51.

Woodring, P. "Big City Superintendent," *Saturday Review*, XLIV (October 21, 1961), pp. 41-42.

IV. STUDIES OF NEW YORK CITY

Association of Assistant Superintendents of New York City. *Study Guide on Policies and Practices Affecting Elementary Schools*. New York: Board of Education, 1952.

Azzarelli, Joseph. *Decision-Making and the Politics of Public Education in New York State: A Research Plan*. Doctoral Dissertation, Teachers College, Columbia University, New York: 1961-62.

Board of Education of the City of New York. *School Planning and Research Division*.

Board of Regents, State of New York. *The Regents Major Legislative Proposals for 1964*.

Brown, Gilbert Clark, *Decision-Making by the Board of Education and Administration of the Springvale, New York Public Schools*. Doctoral Dissertation, Teachers College, Columbia University, New York: 1959-60.

Cohen, Rose N. *The Financial Control of Education in the Consolidated City of*

New York with Special Reference to Interrelations Between the Public School System, the Municipal Government and the State. New York: Bureau of Publications, Teachers College, Columbia University, 1948.

Desegregating the Public Schools of New York City. A Report for the Board of Education of New York City by the State Education Commission Advisory Committee on Human Relations and Community Tensions, May 12, 1964.

Donovan, Bernard. *Implementation of Board Policy on Excellence for the City's Schools.* Report to the Board of Education of the City of New York, April 28, 1965.

Education Commissioner's Committee on Inquiry into Charges of Waste and Extravagance in Construction of School Building in New York City. *School Construction in New York City.* 1951.

Education Law, Section 2553, Subdivision 1, 2, Amended Law 1961.

Education Law, Section 2564, Amended Law 1961.

Files of the Public Education Association.

Fletcher, W. G. *Administrative Patterns in Selected Community Programs in New York City.* New York: Institute of Administrative Research, 1955.

Fletcher, W. G. *Administrative Procedures in School-Community Programs in New York City.* Doctoral project, Teachers College, Columbia University, New York: 1951.

"How Can We Streamline Administration in New York City Schools?" J. Saunders, editor. *New York Society for the Experimental Study of Education Yearbook,* (1961), pp. 1-4.

Kalick, Perry Marvin. *Teacher Assignment in Large Public School Systems.* New York: Report for Teachers College, Columbia University, 1962.

Local Law No. 19, passed by the New York City Council, April 6, 1962.

New York City Department of Education. Bureau of Educational Program Research and Statistics. *Organization of Special Subject Directors.* Publication #128. Prepared by Dr. Samuel McClelland, 1958.

New York City Department of Education. Bureau of Educational Program Research and Statistics. *A Job Analysis and Evaluation of the Position of Principals in New York City.* Publication #184. Prepared by Dr. Samuel McClelland, 1962.

New York City Department of Education. Bureau of Educational Program Research and Statistics. *Special Census of School Population, Summary Tables for the Years 1957-64.*

New York City Department of Education. *General Circular to all Superintendents, Principals, Directors and Heads of Bureaus.* June 5, 1941 to date.

New York City Department of Education, Integration Commission. *Reports to the Commission by the Sub-Commissions on: Guidance, Educational Stimulation and Placement; Educational Standards and Curriculum; Physical Plant and Maintenance; Teacher Assignments and Personnel; and Community Relations and Information.* New York, 1956-57.

New York City Department of Education. *Report to the Regents and the Commissioner of Education of the State of New York and to the Mayor of the City of New York.* Max J. Rubin. As prescribed in Section 7 of Chapter 971 of the laws of New York, enacted August 21, 1962. New York, 1962.

New York City Department of Education. Special Committee on Staff Relations. *Report of the Committee to Study Staff Relations in New York City Schools.* New York, 1952.

New York City Department of Education. *What We Teach: A Review of Curriculum Developments.* Annual Report of the city Superintendent, 1960-61.

New York City Public Schools. *Blueprint for Further Action Toward Quality Integrated Education.* Recommendations of the Superintendent of Schools to the Board of Education, 1965.

New York Herald Tribune. 1962-1965.

"New York Schools Adopt New Programs," *Chicago School Journal,* XLV (January, 1964), p. 187.

The New York Times. 1962-1965.

New York World Telegram and Sun. 1962-1965.

Office of the City Administrator. *Board of Education Organization and Management of School Planning and Construction.* 1959.

"One Dollar in Three; New York's Educational System" *The New York Times, Times Edition Supplement,* May 22, 1964.

Reorganizing Secondary Education in New York City. Education Guidance and Work Committee of the Public Education Association. October, 1963.

Rogers, David. *Unpublished Manuscript on School Integration in New York City.* Center for Urban Education.

Rubin, Julius. *The Role of Teacher Councils in Promoting Democratic Administrations in New York City Public Schools: An Appraisal of the Effectiveness of Teacher Councils in Promoting Staff Participation in the Administration of Their Schools, with Proposals for Increasing Their Effectiveness.* Doctoral Dissertation, New York University: 1956-57.

Sanguinetti, Carmen. *Adapting Science Instruction in New York City Junior High Schools to the Needs of Puerto Rican Background Pupils.* Doctoral Dissertation, Teachers College, Columbia University, New York: 1956-57.

Schinnerer, Mark. *A Report to the New York City Education Department.* New York: 1961.

Sheldon, Eleanor Bernert and Raymond A. Glazier. *Pupils and Schools in New York City: A Fact Book.* New York: Russell Sage Foundation, 1965.

Strayer, George and Louis Yavner. *Administrative Management of the School System of New York City.* Volumes I and II. October, 1951.

Strayer, George. *Guideline for Public School Finance.* Report of Nationwide Survey of State and Local Finance by Phi Delta Kappa, 1963.

Toward Greater Opportunity: A Progress Report from the Superintendent of Schools to the Board of Education Dealing with Implementation of Recommendations of the Commission on Integration. Board of Education of the City of New York, June, 1960.

Swanson, Bert. *School Integration Controversies in New York City.* Bronxville: Institute for Community Studies, Sarah Lawrence College, 1965.

Turner, Richard T. *An Appraisal of the Practices of Science Consultants Operating in the New York City Elementary Schools.* Doctoral Dissertation, Fordham University, 1959-60.

Weitz, Leo. *The High School Principal in New York City: A Study of Executive Responsibility in Theory and Practice.* Doctoral Dissertation, New York University, 1960-61.

Yavner, Louis. *Salaries of School Principals in New York City.* Report to the New York Principals Association, January 14, 1957.

MARILYN GITTELL is an associate professor of political science at Queens College of The City University of New York and director of the college's Institute for Community Studies. She has done research in many aspects of urban and school administration, and recently edited Educating an Urban Society: Implications for Public Policy, to be published later this year by Sage. The present study, which had its origins in a report to the Temporary Commission on City Finances (New York), was completed in December, 1966. Dr. Gittell, who edits Urban Affairs Quarterly, is currently conducting a comparative study of six big-city school systems.